The Ho

-A Memoir-

Susan Acree

Thirsty Zebra
Publishing

Cover Portrait by Cindy Price © Susan Acree

Author Photo © Amber Acree

Photo on Page 10 by Lisa Carter

Lyrics on Page 147-148 © Garth Brooks

Copyright © 2013 by Susan Acree

ISBN-13: 978-1492768494

ISBN-10: 1492768499

*** *In Memory of Race* ***

For my children,

May you know me a bit better.

For my husband,

Thank you for asking me to dance.

Although this is a memoir based on true events and real people, the author has changed the names of some to maintain their privacy.

TABLE OF CONTENTS

PROLOGUE

It's interesting what will click a switch and get you going on something. For me, it was the sudden, tragic loss of my beloved horse, Race. Our connection was so close and our bond so deep that it was beyond understanding to most.

As I reflected back on my years with him, I felt I would never get over the gaping hole in my heart, a void so profound, that it was physically painful. I couldn't see how I would ever be able to get myself past the agony of losing him. And still, my tears flow freely whenever I talk about him.

I thought of all of the wonderful horses I've had in my life. As waves of emotions and memories started to flood in, I remembered how special each one of them had been to me. I began to realize that maybe the best therapy in dealing with the seemingly unbearable loss of Race, would be to relive some of those unique moments of my life that revolved around my sweet horses; good times and bad, happy and sad, triumphant and tragic.

What started as a coping exercise to try to deal with my heartbreak has turned into this book.

So, here are the stories of *the horses I've loved.*

Race and Susan, June 2006
"My Beautiful Boy"

One of the most endearing things about Race was his perpetually relaxed lower lip.

I mentioned this charming characteristic to an old horseman once and he told me, "You know, that's the sign of a truly content horse."

I loved that, it affirmed that he was happy.

A Snapshot of Race . . .

Chapter 1

Across from our home, there was a hayfield and beyond that, a trail on which Race and I had the pleasure of enjoying countless miles and hours together.

Next to the hayfield, was a pasture where Buddy, a charming, black and white speckled donkey resided. Each time we set out to that favored trail, we first had to pass by Buddy's pasture.

To Race, something wasn't quite right about Buddy. Maybe it was his enormous ears, maybe it was because the way that he whinnied was all wrong and not really a whinny at all! Whatever it was, when he would first notice that noisy little donkey, he could see no reason for us to wander too close.

Buddy, on the other hand, was always thrilled to see Race. As we would approach his pasture, Buddy would immediately perk up at the sight of his big handsome horse friend, and then he would come a runnin'. I'm not sure what you call a fairly fast donkey gallop, but as I think about Buddy, the word trollop comes to mind! Race would see those long ears flopping accompanied by that frantic braying and he would seem to say "See ya!" and off we would fly, sideways across the hayfield. Once he finally deemed it safe enough to stop, Race would look back with his ears pricked, neck arched, eyes wide and every muscle in his body trembling. He would then snort and blow at the animated and enthusiastic donkey.

Race was always a *"React first, then stop and ask if he should've panicked once he was a safe distance from the monster"* kind of horse. The monster could be anything from a pile of black garbage bags, to a couple of miniature horses pulling a cart, to an overly friendly donkey named Buddy.

The extraordinary thing about Race, was that in spite of his occasional apprehensiveness, he would follow me to the moon ... if I led him there. He was really brave, when I went first!

I quickly learned that every spring on our first ride by Buddy, it was best to dismount and lead Race up to the fence to let him get reacquainted with the sociable little donkey. He would arch his lovely neck over the top rail of the fence and then give Buddy's ears and nose a good sniff. He'd have to reach way down over the fence because he was so much taller than the diminutive donkey.

After that first ride ritual, Race would look forward to visiting with Buddy. He'd confidently and calmly walk to Buddy's fence and wait while the amiable donkey ran his hardest to get quickly across the pasture to say to his friend, "Heeaw, heeaw!" which, I'm pretty sure translated to "Hello, it's great to see you again, Race!"

*** *2006* ***

I remember patting Race on the neck and telling him I would see him tomorrow. Tomorrow never came for Race. I'll forever question why I didn't stay with him longer at the emergency clinic. Every time I think of that horrible day, I regret not being there with him. I wasted those precious last hours and I could never get them back.

Did he wonder why I left him alone and sick? What was he thinking? Did he feel that I had abandoned him?

I'll never know, and it breaks my heart.

******

OLD SNORT-1961

Chapter 2

My earliest memory on a horse is when I was barely a toddler. My grandparents owned a breathtaking ranch in the Salmon River country of North Central Idaho. I loved going to that ranch. The drive from Pocatello to Salmon took about four hours. I loved spotting deer that were tucked back in the willows along the Lemhi River. I was always on the lookout for horses in the fields of the Angus and Hereford cattle ranches along the way.

The excitement on the drive up the dirt road that led to my grandparent's modest farmhouse was palpable. Their house was painted gray and white with a green shingled roof. There were bright yellow wild roses and fragrant purple and white lilac bushes all around the yard.

Old Snort was Grandpa's work horse. Snort must've had some draft horse in him because I remember he had long, feathery hair on his legs like the Budweiser© Clydesdales. To me, he was huge! But then again, I was only two. I'm not even sure if this first memory is mine, or if I've simply built it from a picture my parents had of me sitting on Snort.

What I *am* sure of, is my deep love for all things related to horses. I believe my passion for horses started with Old Snort on my visits to that enchanting ranch.

I remember my grandpa giving me a squirt of milk directly from the cow's teat, and it being such a shock that it was warm. It seems silly now, but I expected the milk to be ice cold. I also have a wonderful, warm memory of bottle feeding the orphaned lambs. Those baby lambs attacked the bottle nipple as if they were starving. Milk squirted everywhere and dribbled down their chins and onto my hands. I would be so sticky when we went back up to the house from the barns, that with a smile on her lips and a familiar and loved twinkle in her eye, Grandma would ask "How on earth did you get so dirty?!" Then, lovingly she would wash me up, shaking her head and laughing.

As early as any memory I have, I've loved animals of all kinds--except chickens; I don't believe chickens fall into the warm and cuddly category. I think Grandpa also had geese and turkeys, but my love of that ranch was wrapped around the lambs, the calves and, of course, Old Snort.

My mom used to tell me stories about life on the ranch. She had a bright white horse named Topsy. She'd snap her reins together and off they'd run across the fields. She told of how she helped Grandpa get the hay in. I'm sure it was harder work than I could ever imagine, but it sounded wonderful to me. I always wished that I had been around when everyday life involved horses. I would have loved to depend on my horse for work, transportation and recreation.

Old Snort-May 1962
With Grandpa and my brother Dan,
I was not yet two years old
I still have the headstall that Snort is wearing

STICK HORSES-1965

Chapter 3

Most of my early childhood, I felt that I was born in the wrong generation and, for a good part of my life, that I should have been a boy. All of my best friends were boys. My brother seemed to have a much better social life than I did. He had his sports and oodles of friends. He got to go on overnight camping trips with those friends, my friends, but I was a girl and camping with the boys seemed like it was just never going to happen.

I had a great childhood, even if I was a reluctant girl. We lived on Park Avenue, not in NYC, but in Pocatello, Idaho. Our next door neighbors were the Price family. For years, Chad and Marilyn Price and their children were part of our everyday lives. All of my boy friends . . . they were all Price boys.

First there was Casey, he was the oldest boy in the family, and oh so cool. He was ten when I was six. Rod was next, and he was eight, the same age as my brother, Dan. Paul was my age and my best friend, we were inseparable. Chuck was the youngest, but he was too young to hang with the big kids, he was just the baby brother that tagged along sometimes, but was with our moms most of the time.

Wendy was the oldest of the Price children and didn't often take part in our childhood games. She did have some great record albums, though. Once, I remember being in her room while she was listening to "Blowing in the Wind." I can't recall if it was Peter, Paul and Mary or Bob Dylan. At the time, I had no interest in singers or bands; they had nothing to do with horses. But that day, I remember how Wendy made me feel a little bit grown up, letting me listen to records in her room with all of her teen idols smiling at us from posters on the wall.

This chapter is called Stick Horses right? Paul had two. A stick horse is basically a broom handle about three feet long with a horse head, usually made of cloth or vinyl, attached to one end. One of Paul's stick horses was tan and of course his name was Trigger, named after Roy Rogers' magnificent Palomino horse. Paul always got Trigger. The other one was candy apple red, who wants to ride a bright red horse? ... But, he was the one Paul let me ride. I don't recall ever naming my red horse, seems kind of mean now, I'm sure he didn't want to be red.

We rode for miles and miles up and down the street. We thought we lived in the greatest place on earth. We could ride our horses to Alameda park, just at the end of our block and be transformed into real cowboys. We'd gallop across the grass and through the trees without a care in the world. All of the neighbors knew us. They'd say "There go Susan and Paul again." I'm pretty sure we were celebrities with our trick riding and jumping obstacles along the sidewalk. We raced too, and Paul probably always won, but that's only because he had Trigger, the greatest horse ever, in the eyes of a five-year-old girl whose life revolved around horses, real and make believe.

Years later Paul had been living in Los Angeles, training racehorses at Los Alamitos Race Track. Paul took his folks, *my horse parents*, Chad and Marilyn, through the Roy Rogers Museum on one of their visits. They called and told me that they'd brought me a gift from Paul. When I stopped by their home, they presented me with my own Trigger. His head is made of yellow cotton material with a white felt blaze on his face. His mane is trimmed white yarn and he whinnies when I press his ear. When they handed him to me, they told me, "When Paul saw this stick horse he said, I have to get this for Sue. She always wanted Trigger." That stick horse is proudly hitched in my room, every once in a while I'll squeeze his ear and think of Paul.

No one called me Sue except for the Price boys. I was always Susan to the rest of the world. I don't know why it didn't bother me; it just sounded right coming from them.

My parents said they almost named me Dale, and when I was little, I wished they had. Dale was a boy's name, my dad's actually, but they were thinking more like Dale Evans, Roy's wife, but how could've they known I'd grow up to be a cowgirl. I always took exception to that label—cowgirl, pfft! I was a *horse* girl, and I didn't want anything to do with cows, with their perpetually snotty, slimy noses and ceaselessly fly covered hides. I admit the calves were cute, but adult cows and steers were not my idea of soft and huggable pets.

We spent a few more years living on Park next to the Prices. Then, they moved to their Grandpa Harry's Quarter Horse farm. Chad built their house with a lot of help from family and friends. All of us helped build that house. The big boys hauled cinder bricks and the heavier materials. As for the little kids, we hauled buckets and buckets of mortar, or mud as they called it. Chad and Marilyn finished the basement first, so they could move in and work on the rest of the house while they lived in it. It was a large house with six bedrooms, but only three in the basement, so for a while the boys all shared one room, while Wendy had her own, one of the perks of being the only girl and the oldest.

My dad, who was an accomplished carpenter, volunteered to build all of the cabinetry in the house. It was an enormous job, but back in those days, friends did big things for their friends.

As they finished building the rest of the house, I spent countless, joyous hours at the farm. There were three other Price families that lived out there. Grandpa Harry and Grandma Gerti had their modest little house at the front of the property. In later years, they turned their basement into an apartment that many a grandchild lived in while transitioning to adulthood. Across the lane from them, Chad's sister and her family had a nice, white brick house. At the top of the lane, one of Chad's brothers and his family had a little reddish-pink brick house that overlooked the back pastures. Chad and Marilyn built across the lane from them. The Price farm was a magical place for me. It was everything I imagined a horse ranch should be. The barn had the sweet aroma of straw filled stalls and the rustling of horses milling about in them. I loved walking down the barn aisle and petting the horses, giving each one kisses on their soft, velvety noses. The pastures were full of horses and ponies, the hay shed was always filled with fragrant alfalfa, and to this young horse lover, it was heaven on earth.

As parents go, I hit the jackpot. My mom and dad were the greatest. They supported my brother and me in all of our endeavors. They spent countless hours sitting on hard, cold bleacher benches overlooking dusty arenas, crisp green football fields and stinky high school basketball courts. My dad, with his quiet way, seemed faultless to me. I loved that when we walked together, he would always hold my hand. He never uttered a cuss word, but boy if he said "Dagnabbit!" we knew he was irritated. His discipline was a stern word when needed, but those times were rare; my brother and I just did not want to disappoint him.

My mom was a rock. She was feisty at work as an instructor at the University and always a professional. She fought for what she thought was right. Her love for us was unwavering and undeniable. She was the ultimate Mamma Bear. One never wanted to see the side of her that emerged if you wronged her children. Mom was friendly and greeted all with a smile. Everyone who knew her, especially her students, would always exclaim when they found out she was my mother "Oh, I just love Mrs. Deagle!"

Mom and Dad were the kind of parents every child could only wish for, and they were mine.

STAR-1969

Chapter 4

Star, my very special first horse

As Dad worked on the house, I got to spend every spare minute at the farm, surrounded by horses. The more time I spent at the farm, the more obsessed I became with having my own horse. I remember leaving notes all over the house, pleading my case for a horse of my own. I recall some of my parent's friends telling them, "Just get her a horse, she'll outgrow it in a couple of years." Yeah, right, forty plus years later. . .

Well, obviously, I eventually wore my folks down and we started looking for a horse. I was in Campfire Girls and went to summer camp every year; there was always a string of trail horses for the campers to ride. I spent every second they would allow, hanging around the corrals. I could never get enough of just being near horses. Before I left for camp, I expressed my concern to my parents that they would buy a horse while I was gone, this worried me, I knew I wanted to choose my own horse. My concerns turned out to be well founded; the day they picked me up from camp they surprised me with the news that Star was mine. I was a little disappointed at first because they'd done just what I was afraid they would. However, that feeling soon melted away as the reality of having my own horse sunk in. It turned out that Chad had given Star to us in exchange for all of my dad's work on the cabinets. Also, part of the deal, was that she'd still live on the farm and they would continue to feed her and take care of her, because after all, we still lived in town on Park Ave. As a nine-year-old, I had a whopping $35.00 in my savings account. This, as luck would have it, was the *exact* amount I needed to pay dad for my first horse, Star.

Star came with a saddle and bridle and everything I needed to be a horse owner. But, with our parents always working on the house, we kids had to fend for ourselves when it came to play time. Thus, saddling horses was just too much work, so we simply rode bareback. Of course, having a Shetland pony, I was on the littlest horse, so it was quite easy for me to get on. The boys were all destined to be jockeys so swinging up on 16-hand quarter horses was never a problem for them. A hand is four inches. Horses are measured from their withers to the ground in hands. The horse's withers are at the bottom of the mane at the tallest point where the back meets the neck, over the shoulders.

Paul had a cute little horse named Swisher. She was the foal (baby) of Star, a sorrel (brownish red) Shetland pony with a gray mane and tail. Chad bred Star to a Quarter Horse stud to get the little half horse; Swisher was the perfect size for kids. She was almost black, and I remember she was just such a nice little horse. Petite and a lovely mover, she just floated along the ground.

Rod's horse was Happy Appy, a beautiful strawberry Appaloosa. She was the good horse that anybody could ride. I remember one day before I had Star, Rod and I were loping across the field, riding double, bareback of course. Rod tried to turn Appy to circle around the field but she thought we should go straight to the shade tree ahead of us. As we leaned into the turn, she went straight and we slid off her side, both of us landing in horse manure. Rod came up spitting. He was not a happy boy. It is funny that of all of my memories, this is one that stands out, falling off a horse, with one of my cool boy-friends into a pile of horse poop, huh...

When you own a horse farm, every horse is for sale at one time or another; at least that was Chad's philosophy. Casey seemed to get the brunt of that reality during our growing up years. Every time he would get a horse trained pretty well and start to get attached, Chad would sell it. I remember he had a horse called Pop Top.

He was a racehorse of course, but in the off season, he was a kid horse. We used to ride down the road and across the highway to the Portneuf River. This was not a big river, but it had a significant enough current that the boys would tether Star and me to the big horses to make sure we didn't get carried away. Once across the river, there were plenty of mountains and foothills to climb, and dirt roads to race on, but our favorite game was making use of the cattle catch pens that were over there. We'd let the horses loose in the corral and then sit on the fence and jump onto our own horse as it went by down the chute.

Our safety riders were Rod and Casey, since they were the oldest. They'd sit at the end of the fence and catch our horses if we happened to miss. I only recall one time when a horse got loose; I don't think he was too anxious to leave the rest of the herd, so when he came out of the end of the chute rider-less, he just turned back, trotted over and stopped by the fence where the other horses were still corralled. On one particular ride across the river, we were all at the gate ready to go home except Casey. As we were waiting, all of a sudden we heard him yelling "Open the gate, open the gate!" Well, we didn't. Did I mention Pop Top was a racehorse? When we all got ahead of him, Pop Top took off after us at full throttle. We didn't open the gate, which was probably a good thing. He may not have stopped until he got home! To get home, he would've had to cross a broken down old bridge, then the railroad tracks, and finally the highway on his way.

Pop Top did an imitation of a sports car sliding to a stop in gravel. He ran up to the fence and at the last moment, slammed on his brakes and turned to miss the fence; unfortunately, Casey wound up in the dirt. He was furious with us and covered in thick, powdery dirt that made him look like a dust ghost. He may have been black and blue for a few days, but I still think we did the right thing by not opening the gate.

Since I'm telling stories in which Casey is black and blue, I have one more. The horses were, for the most part, all kept together in big pastures. Casey went out to catch his horse in the herd. Sometimes you could take grain, but that was quite risky, since horses can get pretty pushy when treats are involved. Anyway, when Casey went down to get his horse, he told me to stand Star at the gateway to keep the horses from running through if he didn't catch his right away. Evidently, there was no gate. Remember, Star was just little, and at nine, I was already almost too big for her. We were doing our best to imitate a roadblock, but as Casey put his arms around his horse to put the halter on, the entire herd took off, full blast, of course. The black and blue part came when he didn't let go! So there he was, hanging from his horse's neck and being stepped on with every stride, heading straight for us. Star and I might have been small and young, respectively, but we knew enough to get out of the way when a bunch of big horses was running at us. Casey finally let go and his folks came out to assess the damage on his beat up body. I started to go over to apologize for not holding the herd. I remember Paul coming over and telling me, "Unless you want to see Casey with his pants off, you probably should wait a while." I did. I waited a long while. I was feeling so bad about not doing my job. I was afraid Casey would be mad at me forever. Somewhere in the course of time he forgave me. Casey broke his leg in that horse stampede. One of many, many broken bones that the Price boys suffered...they did break easily and often.

We played all sorts of games on horseback, and one of our favorites was tag. It was an elaborate kind of tag, though. We had not only the players but also our "horse city police," "school bus" and "taxi." Happy Appy was the school bus or taxi, depending on how many kids she had lined up on her back. She was a big, long horse, so if she just had one or two she was a taxi. If she had three or four, she was a school bus. China Babe was the police horse. She was a beautiful gray mare. If somebody broke the law in our game of tag, whoever was riding her could dole out the penalty. China Babe loved to back up, in fact, if Chad ever caught us over-using her reverse gear, we'd have to put her away. By the way, China Babe was Happy Appy's mom (dam).

Another of our fun activities was the July 24th Pioneer Day Parade; back in those days, it went right by our house and ended up at Alameda Park. We'd dress up our horses and proudly ride in the parade and wave as if everyone came out just to see us. The Prices had a dog named Lucky; he lived up to his name by surviving many horse and car-related accidents. During the parade he'd sit on Appy's butt, right behind Rod, I guess she was also the "dog horse."

My first parade on Star was memorable. My mom helped me sew little ruffles for Star to wear on her ankles. They kept falling down too far and she kept stepping on them with her front hooves, so we had to slide them up above her knees. They were white with pink pompoms around the bottom and I wore a white shirt and a pink tie to match. After the parade we'd end up in our back yard, horses and all, for a picnic before we headed to the park for a day of fun and games.

Susan and Star ready for the parade
Bareback of course, with Paul on Swisher behind

That year at the county fair, there were activities and events planned before the rodeo. The ribbon pull was the one Star and I entered. Since we didn't have a horse trailer yet, we just loaded Star in the back of the pickup and I sat back there with her on the drive up to the fairgrounds. She was a great little horse, kind of a *"been there, done that"* pony. Once we got to the fairgrounds, we unloaded her, got her saddled and bridled and headed to the arena.

The object of the event was to run down on your horse, jump off, grab a ribbon from a goat's tail, get back on and run back to the start/finish line. I was really good at going fast, so I was way ahead of the competition when I got to the goat. The ribbon came off quite easily so all I had to do was get back on and run home. As mentioned before, saddles were rarely used items, so I had very little experience getting on one in a hurry. Not surprisingly, I couldn't seem to get my foot in the stirrup. I should have just jumped on and ignored the saddle, but I didn't and I lost; quite devastating to a nine-year-old at her first rodeo. Oh well, it was fun while I was winning!

That one event was probably the precursor to my eventual love of speed events, such as barrel racing and pole bending. I never did get into goat tying, I always said it seemed silly to jump off a perfectly good running horse, but it was probably a deep seeded fear of not being able to get back on.

When my parents decided it was time for me to have my own horse, they thought it was only fair that my brother, Dan, get a horse of his own, too. They bought a little yearling filly. She was born in August, so we aptly named her Summertime. A filly is a young female horse. She was a homely little thing when we got her, but she grew into a beauty. My brother did the initial riding with the help of the Price boys.

Meanwhile, I was the happiest I had ever been, adoring and doting on Star. It didn't take long for Dan to lose interest in having a horse. Because he was always so busy with sports, he didn't need another activity to fill his life. I did. Having a horse changed me from an extremely introverted girl, who hated all things girly . . . dresses, dolls, playing house . . . to a not quite so introverted girl, who was now a horse owner with a newly defined purpose in life.

From the very beginning, *my horses were the foundation of my being.*

When I first saw Race in the field next to his mom, Racy Rachel Lynn, I knew immediately he was going to be my next horse....

When I walked up to him out in the pasture and gave him a rub on the neck and a scratch on the rump, we instantly had a connection.

It was as if fate intended for us to be together.

******

KANDY-1970

Chapter 5

Susan and Kandy

As I said before, I was almost too big for Star from the beginning, so after a year it was evident that I needed to up-size. Dan wasn't quite ready to give up Summertime, so when Chad said he'd found a cute, three-year-old half Arabian, half Quarter Horse for $75, we decided to take a look. Kandy was a pretty fancy looking horse with a big blaze and three above-the-knee white stockings. She was a bright sorrel with a flaxen mane and tail. We bought her and brought her "home" to the Price farm. Chad and the boys helped me train her, I don't recall her ever bucking with me, but I was only ten and maybe they took the bucks out when I wasn't around. I didn't have Kandy very long, and I don't recollect why I sold her, but she was the horse that I took on the famous "Overnight" ride, so she gets her own chapter.

As I mentioned earlier, I always thought my brother had a much better life than I did. The basis for this thought was this single fact: he got to go on overnight camping trips with the boys and I was never allowed. One afternoon, a simple phone call from Chad gave me the opportunity to go on an unforgettable adventure that changed all that.

I believe it was a Thursday and all he said was "Can you be ready to go on an "overnighter" by Friday afternoon?" I couldn't believe it! Evidently, he had already talked with my parents about it, because my mom immediately clapped her hands together and said "We better get to packing." We went to the grocery store first. We bought things like little cans of fruit and pudding. I remember the pudding well. It became one of *the* memories of that trip.

I got a brand new sleeping bag-a sleeping bag that I still have 40 years later; it was obviously a great bag. We didn't have any saddlebags, so I used some old ones that Chad had. The afternoon arrived; we got to the farm and started trying on the tack to make sure everything fit just right. I remember Rod telling me we had to switch saddles after the first day so the horses wouldn't get sore. He said I'd use his saddle the second day, so I should try it on Kandy to make sure it fit all right. What happened next was one of those lessons I learned with horses and never forgot; and then passed down to my own children and grandchildren.

My saddle did not have a back cinch, thus being my excuse for forgetting about the back cinch on Rod's saddle before I pulled it off Appy to put it on Kandy. Big mistake! Once I started pulling it off, I realized I had forgotten to unbuckle the back cinch and there was no way I could get that heavy saddle back up on her. The saddle slid around her until it was hanging under her belly, and even a good old horse is going to go a little crazy when she has a saddle hanging under her. She took off bucking "like a bat out of hell!" to quote someone who had obviously seen a horse with a saddle under her belly. Did I mention that this was a brand-new saddle? It was, and it wasn't even Rod's, it was his mom's. We were going to break it in for her *real good*. Yup! Well, after a couple of good hard bucks, the leather of the back cinch tore out where it was buckled and fell off Appy. Fortunately, there was not a tremendous amount of damage done to horse or saddle, but enough to send a ten-year-old into a huge guilt trip. I felt so stupid; I just knew the boys were thinking I wasn't old enough to be going on this ride. I think Rod was a little mad at me, but when everything calmed down they were all pretty nice about it, even Marilyn. They just told me to *always* remember to unbuckle the loose back cinch *first* before the main front cinch. Lesson learned. To this day, I've never made that mistake again and every time I see someone un-cinch the front cinch first, they get my story.

So, the tack was ready and the saddlebags were packed...with more than just my pudding and other goodies. We loaded the horses, said goodbye to the moms and we were off. Here I was, on my first overnighter, just me and the boys. Our group included Chad of course, and his brother-in-law, they were the grownups; and the four boys, Casey, Rod, Paul, and their younger cousin who rode Star, and me.

A side note about Star, when I outgrew her and moved on to Kandy, we just gave her back to the Price family. Chuck, the youngest, was only three or four years old at the time, and well, all of the Price children just started out on Star. Years later, Casey's two oldest children also learned to ride on Star. One morning they found her feet up in the water trough, not a nice vision I know. She must've gone quickly; Chad and Casey thought she probably had a heart attack. She had to have been close to 30 years old.

Now, back to the "Overnighter." We hauled the horses up to the mountains. We were probably only 20 or 30 miles out of Pocatello, but it seemed like a long way. Mom, Dad and Marilyn followed us up so that they could take the two horse trailers back to where we would be coming out the next day.

We headed up the trail to Harkness Canyon near McCammon. It was beautiful, in an Idaho way. Pine trees, fragrant sagebrush and tall meadow grass that swayed in the breeze. I've always loved the smell of the mountains; fresh and crisp with a pinch of dust and the familiar aroma of evergreens. Someone should make a dusty mountain trail scented candle! We were going to ride through Beckler Meadows the first day and then end up riding out Inman Canyon the next. So off we went, on the biggest adventure of my life, up to that point. We rode and talked and laughed and rode. I learned that "bum fodder" was a leaf used for toilet paper if that was all that was available. I saw a man blow his nose without a hankie and without even breaking stride! I realized, with even more conviction that I was the wrong gender every time we had to stop for a pee break and I had to hike up and hide behind a tree or bush, while all the boys waited for me. We went up steep trails and down mild ones.

Toward the end of the first day, we were strung out along the trail, when something happened behind me. The trail was fairly narrow and made a sharp 'S' curve. Chad warned Casey to pay attention to his young horse. Poor Casey, again, with a new horse! Young, inexperienced horses tend to gawk around and not watch where they're putting their feet. This particular horse, a young mare named Andee, was doing just that. She saw the horses ahead of her that had already passed the curve, so to her, they seemed to be just across the hillside. So, instead of watching the trail and following it to catch up with the other horses, she simply stepped off the trail. That one misstep started their unplanned slide down the hill. Amazingly, Casey was able to bail off before the mare started rolling. Of course, it was Casey's horse that was carrying my little pudding cups. "Oh no! Not the pudding!" Fortunately, Casey and his horse survived that ill-fated ordeal; the pudding was not so lucky!

When we reached a small, quiet meadow surrounded by towering pine trees, Chad announced "This looks like a perfect place to set up camp." The meadow had tall, thick grass that would make a nice, comfy place to sleep. So, we stopped for the night and unsaddled and removed the saddlebags, canteens and sleeping bags from the horses. By the flickering light of the campfire, we realized we now had chocolate flavored saddlebags, and if we wanted pudding we were going to have to scrape it out of the canvas bags. Rod was livid. He'd been looking forward to that chocolate pudding all day. Years later, when reminiscing with Rod about the "overnighter," he said that's about all he remembered of the trip. He recalled being so mad at Casey for allowing his "stupid horse" to ruin our pudding! I'm sure that Chad fixed some sort of dinner, I really don't remember. Regardless, I was having the time of my life! Nothing mattered; not the smashed pudding cups, not the shyness, not the all too often perceived absence of a little girl playing with dolls, not the seemingly insurmountable shadow of my brother, and not even the heartbreaking times that I got left behind. I was up in the mountains with all of my best friends, the man that I came to love as my "horse dad" and of course, all of those horses.

As we got ready for bed, we unrolled our sleeping bags on the soft meadow grass. My brand new sleeping bag now had horse sweat stains all over the outside flap. Even after getting the bag cleaned, the faded sweat spot remained. Every time I use my sleeping bag, I see that discoloration and love remembering the momentous occasion from which it came. We used our saddle blankets for pillows, scooted into our sleeping bags in our clothes and whispered into the night until the excitement and exertion of the day finally caught up to us and we slept.

Kids never want to get up in the morning, so Chad had to roust us out of our bags with orders to get our horses taken care of. As soon as the sun was up, so were we! He told us "Nobody gets breakfast until the horses have been fed and watered." That was a lesson I passed on to my own children when they went on to participate in 4-H. Stalls cleaned, horses fed, watered and walked, and then they could come back to the tent, camper, or trailer and have their own breakfast.

That morning after we ate, we saddled up and headed down the canyon toward the spot where the trailers were parked. We had to cross a few creeks, of which not all of the horses were good. Some of them just plodded through, others stopped and pawed and splashed until everyone around them was soaked, and others still, had to be persuaded to cross, usually with willing horses in front of and behind them.

Fortunately, we didn't have any more misadventures with the horses; we just enjoyed the beautiful outdoors and the wonder of nature. We ran up the trails, and down hills, we chased cows and each other, playing tag and follow the leader. In my mind, it couldn't get any better than this, I was living my dream. At the time, we were just kids on a grand adventure, in later years, I'd think back on that weekend with the happiest of feelings.

We made it back to the trailers, unsaddled and loaded up, some bruised, most dusty, and all happy. Although we were exhausted, we chattered and laughed about our adventure as we drove home. I am so grateful to Chad and the boys for including me. It is one of the most cherished memories of my life.

The true significance of that trip has become exceptionally clearer through the years. The fact that I was included and accepted on that one particular adventure proved that I was valued in the eyes of others. Maybe someday, I would feel worthy in my own eyes.

SUMMERTIME-1971

Chapter 6

Susan and Summertime at the State Fair in 1972

Summertime was my brother Dan's horse. She was a registered P.O.A. P.O.A. stands for Pony of the Americas. When we first bought her, for the tidy sum of $50.00, she was a yearling and honestly, just a plain little brown horse. As she matured, the brown turned to a beautiful dappled gray. Her mane and tail turned bright white and she had perfect conformation and a heart of gold.

After the initial excitement and novelty of having his own horse wore off, Dan realized he really wasn't interested in being a horse owner. With baseball in the summer, football in the fall, basketball in the winter, and track in the spring, he just didn't have time for horses.

I think the final decision to put his horse days behind him came after one particular trail ride. We'd taken our dog, Cindy, and somewhere along the trail on our way home, she had fallen behind. Dan noticed she wasn't with us anymore and was frantic to go back and look for her. When we finally found her, she was so worn out and dehydrated that Chad had to carry her with him on his horse the rest of the ride back. Dan had been so distraught over Cindy's condition that I think he somehow attached that distress to horses.

I believe Chad had someone interested in buying Kandy, because *"every horse is always for sale,"* so I sold her and inherited Summertime, Summer for short. She was the perfect size for me at the time. Star had been too small and Kandy was a bit tall, so Summertime, like the baby bear's bed, was just right.

It was with Summer that I started my 4-H horse career. Paul and his cousins had joined a club with a crotchety older lady as the leader. I should be more kind. That woman actually spent a better part of her life giving her time to several generations of youngsters and their horses of various sizes, shapes and breeds. But, how do I say this? She was just cranky most of the time. I guess her patience was depleted after so many years of dealing with wild kids on half trained horses. That group's practice time didn't fit with my parents' work schedule, so I wasn't able to join that club. So, my first year in 4-H, I didn't use a horse. I joined a non-horse club and did projects in cooking and sewing, much to my mother's frustration. Teaching an 11-year-old how to sew is not an easy task. I do thank her for it though. Throughout my life I've used my moderate sewing skills to make Halloween costumes for my children, matching mother and son flannel shirts, and a few doggy coats. I am actually fairly competent at general alterations and mending tasks.

In addition to cooking and sewing, I entered a dog project that first year. I used our family dog, Cindy. She was a mutt, but she looked like a small version of a Gordon Setter.

Cindy in 1971

I loved doing the obedience training with her. I remember going to practice and coming home to try to improve Cindy's response to the commands we had learned. One particularly difficult one for us was the 'recall.' When I would say "Cindy, come!" she would think I was mad at her and cower. My mom worked with her a little bit and discovered that if I just said "Here, Cindy" she gladly and energetically responded. That first year, Cindy and I did okay, but nothing spectacular. I remember one dog show, we made a mistake and I was feeling sorry for myself. Cindy lay down by me and tried to put her paw on my hand and I brushed it away. My parents reminded me that she had done her best and she needed reassurance that I still loved her. I still feel ashamed over that little tantrum. Yet another uncomfortable and sensitive life lesson.

The next year, we found a horse 4-H club that I could join. The only problem was that they practiced at the fairgrounds and we did not yet have a horse trailer. We decided it'd be safe enough for me to ride to the fairgrounds if Mom drove behind me in the car. We set out on a route that took us to the front gate of the fairgrounds. It had taken us over an hour to get there, only to then realize that the front gate was locked and I had to continue my trek all the way around to the backside of the grounds, which took another half-hour. I was late and tired that first time but it was worth it. I was finally in 4-H with my horse.

I met a girl that also rode to 4-H at the fairgrounds. Her name was Jane and she had a little black and white paint pony. She was older than I, but very thin and petite, so she still fit her pony, 7-Up Sergeant. 7-Up Sergeant had a long career as a show pony for several kids in town. He'd move from home to home and as one young rider would outgrow him, he would be passed on to a new family and train another. Those kinds of horses are rare and priceless.

Jane and I made plans to ride together from then on and she showed me a shorter way to get to 4-H practice. This was great because it gave me some independence and my mom a little more free time since she no longer had to follow. Jane was in a different club, but it didn't matter. Our two clubs met the same days in different arenas at the fairgrounds, so it worked out perfectly.

My club was awesome. My leader's name was Keith and he had two sons, Ross and Hunter. I was 11 and just starting to notice boys. They were both so cute. In later years the older one, Ross, would actually work for my dad. He grew up to be just as handsome as a man as he had been cute as a teenager when we were in 4-H together. We had our membership meetings out at their house. It was a long way across town because they lived south of Pocatello and we lived north. But again, it was worth it. One night at the end of our meeting, I was telling Keith about something neat that Summertime had done. All of a sudden he started gasping for breath. His face flushed and he clutched his chest. He hollered for Ross and I fearfully backed away. The panic I felt was new to me, and I didn't know how to react. It was a very scary moment and I just wanted to retreat from the scene.

Keith was okay that night, but ended up dying a few years later of heart failure. He was far too young. At the time, I didn't think of how losing their dad would affect his sons' entire lives or that their children would miss out on having an amazing grandfather. I did however start to realize that my heroes were mortal and that life did not go on forever. We all eventually experience loss.

The culmination of all of the weeks of practice was the County Fair in Downey. We would load up and haul our horses the 40 miles to the South Bannock County Fairgrounds. When we arrived, we would unload, find our assigned row of stalls in the barns and get our horses settled in the narrow stalls, which would be their home for the next week. The facilities, by today's standards, were quite bleak. The barns did not have box stalls where the horses could move around and lie down if they wanted. They were tie-in stalls, just wide enough for the horses to fit, with a feed trough at their heads for hay and usually, just a rope behind their tails. If the horse was a kicker, he would have a gate at his rear and a red ribbon in his tail. We'd take the horses out of their stalls several times a day to water them at the common water trough located between the barns. Like I said, the accommodations were pretty meager, but at the time, they seemed just fine.

At this fair, it was either camp or sleep in the barn. So, out came our modest, tiny tent trailer. When it was folded up, it looked like a little red rectangular box. When it was set up, the tent was unfolded on top of the base. It had a bunk on each side and a little table in the middle. It wasn't fancy and smelled like slightly musty canvas, but at least we had a place to get out of the sun, away from the bugs and to sleep. Mom and I put our sleeping bags on the thin mattress pads on the bunks and were plenty comfy.

We had shopped long and hard for my show outfits. Money was tight, but we came up with a red shirt and red jeans that matched perfectly and looked great on my pretty gray horse. Looking back on that outfit, it was an awful lot of red. I later learned that having pants in a contrasting color to your horse allows the judge to see even the slightest movement of the legs. So, black jeans on a black horse or in my case light colored jeans on my gray horse would have been better choice as a first year competitor. Older, more experienced riders, who had absolute confidence in their proficiency in the saddle, would welcome the sharp contrast as an opportunity to show the judges their exceptionally quiet legs and polished, smooth and poised riding ability.

The first class of the fair was always showmanship, and I was excited to get dressed in my red outfit. I was all ready to go, and headed toward the barn to get Summertime, but as soon as Hunter saw me, he told me we all had to wear the club uniform, a plain white shirt and blue jeans for showmanship. Even though I was a little disappointed that my colorful outfit had been vetoed, I hopped back into the trailer for a quick change. Showmanship is a non-riding class. The horse is put through some basic maneuvers such as walk, trot, halt and pivot by the handler on the ground. The concept is that you are showing your horse to the judge. You should never stand between the judge and your horse thus obstructing his view. There are specific ways and times that you move from one side of your horse to the other to keep the judge's line of sight clear. The anticipation of the planned and rehearsed moves always caused my stomach to flip flop. Your horse is also supposed to stand "squared up" for the judge's inspection. "Squared up" simply means that if a line was drawn from hoof to hoof to hoof to hoof in the dirt; the resulting shape would be a square or more precisely a rectangle. Another aspect of the showmanship judging is based on how clean and properly groomed your horse is and also how his halter and lead rope are fitted. The actual name of the class is Fitting and Showing. I learned a lot in showmanship that year; I just didn't understand the purpose and intent yet. I was determined to practice and improve by next year.

Even though I wanted to do better in the halter classes, it was the riding classes that I looked forward to and were the most fun. I competed in Western Pleasure, Bareback Equitation, Barrel Racing and Pole Bending.

Western Pleasure and Bareback Equitation classes are events that require the rider to demonstrate his ability to put the horse through simple maneuvers. The horse should be obedient and calm and have a pleasant demeanor about him. A happy horse is a willing horse. He must walk, trot and canter or lope at a comfortable speed in both directions. While in the canter, the horse must also maintain the correct lead, which in these events is defined as the hind foot to the inside of the arena striking the ground first, then the inside front and outside hind hit the ground. As the horse is cantering it appears that the inside front foot is leading.

Susan and Summertime
Our first Western Equitation Class
Bannock County Fair, 1971

As I continued to practice to perfect my riding skills, I focused on what I had been taught; shoulders back, chin up, and heels down. As I steadily improved as a rider, I learned to rely on the feel and connection with my horse to attain a balanced and comfortable seat.

The speed events were my absolute favorites. I always loved going fast; from my first exciting, albeit disappointing rodeo on Star to all of the races we had run through the fields at the ranch, jumping ditches and kicking up dust.

Riding fast horses is addictive.

Barrel racing is a thrilling speed event. It has been described as a *controlled* runaway horse race. As shown in the diagram, three 55 gallon barrels are set up in a triangle in the arena.

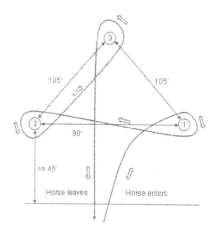

Barrel Pattern

The rider runs her horse into the arena at top speed. Her time starts when her horse's nose crosses the start/finish line. The rider can elect to go to either the left or right barrel first. This decision is usually based on which way the horse turns best. There are either two turns to the left or two turns to the right, depending on which way you start. The above diagram shows a full set of barrels, but depending on the size of the arena, the barrel pattern measurements can be adjusted. As she approaches the first barrel, the rider must rate her horse. This means she must ask her horse to set up for the turn. Although still running, the horse must rate, or slow down, just enough to make a smooth, close turn and then power on to the next barrel. Upon completing the turn at the third and final barrel, the rider urges her horse to finish the pattern at his absolute top speed. The time stops when the horse's nose crosses the start/finish line. Because barrel races are usually decided by hundredths of a second, an electronic-eye timer is used.

   If a barrel is tipped over, it results in a 5 second penalty. I cannot begin to describe the sick feeling when a barrel falls over.   That awful sinking sensation in the pit of your stomach is the same whether the barrel falls from being knocked down when the horse shoulders into it, or when you painfully catch it with your leg mid turn, or when you kick it over with your boot as you are accelerating to the next barrel. Some girls even try to catch the falling barrel and push it back up in the split second that it is happening, but that effort is rarely successful. Think of it like this. From across the room, you see a glass of red wine being tipped over and spilled onto your new light cream carpet. It happens in an instant, but plays in your mind in slow motion, you make a diving effort to catch it, but to no avail because the rim is just barely out of the reach of your saving fingertips. When the scene goes back to real time, you just added five seconds to your barrel run.

   Pole bending is also an exhilarating and precise speed event. Unlike the barrels, pole bending pattern measurements must be the same at every event. There are six poles that are made of 1 ½ inch diameter by six-foot-long PVC pipe. Each pole is secured vertically in a weighted rubber base to keep it perfectly perpendicular to the ground.

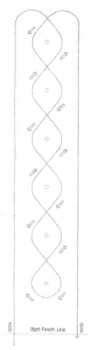

Pole Bending Pattern

The first pole is set 21 feet from the start/finish line. The next pole is 21 feet from the first and then the subsequent four poles are spaced 21 feet apart in a straight line.

The rider enters the arena at a run, starting the electronic timer at the start/finish line. She must run to the farthest end pole and turn tightly around it 180 degrees. From there, she must weave, still maintaining the fastest speed possible, between each pole. At the closest end pole she again performs a tight turn and weaves back through the poles. At the far end pole, she makes one final 180 degree turn and runs for the finish line. Knocking down a pole is not only painful but costly. Each pole tipped results in a five second penalty.

We also had a play day during the fair that wasn't a competition, it was just for fun. We had silly games like the egg and spoon race where you had to ride around the arena at the different gaits carrying an egg in a spoon. The goal was to be the last one to still have your egg. There was also the bareback dollar class. It involved riding our horses bareback and placing a dollar bill under one thigh. As the class progressed and the participants lost their dollars, they would ride to the center of the arena and stand in a line. If competition was tough, the judge would have the last few riders move the dollar farther and farther down their leg, sometimes by the time it was to the knee, the winner would emerge, but a few times I recall the last two contestants having to hold that dollar bill under the calf of their leg. The class would continue until only one person still had their dollar, then he or she would get to keep all of the dollars!

I came away from my first County Fair with lots of ribbons--probably not a lot of blue ones--but I still had such an exciting and fun time.

The other notable part of the County Fair experience was the social life. The boys in 4-H always seemed to be carrying around their lariats. They'd rope the girls, and they were quite the showoffs. I think they just wanted to get close enough to have to *unrope* us. The really cool future cowboys roped the girls' feet like the heelers in team roping. They would just lay that rope in front of us and darn it, we just couldn't miss stepping in that loop. The nights were spent flirting and giggling and walking around the fairgrounds hoping to spot the special boy you had your eye on. Then the leaders and parents would herd us all back to our tents and campers and we'd try to get some sleep, but the excitement took a while to wear off and it always seemed like I'd no sooner get my eyes closed than someone was waking me up.

One year, the fair overlapped the day my mom had to go back to work at the University. So, a friend and my cousin came to Downy to spend the night with me. The girls went to bed at a reasonable hour, but I was visiting with the boy who had caught my attention that year. I didn't come back to the camper until the wee hours of the morning and they were sure I was going to be in big trouble. I guess they didn't tattle, because I never received the dreaded "*talkin' to.*"

By the time the State Fair rolled around, about a month later, the attraction had evidently faded. When I ran into *the boy* in one of the livestock barns he simply said "Hi Ugly." Wow! That was a quick, but potent lesson in the behaviors of adolescents. Not knowing if he was joking or if he really thought I was ugly, I reacted, as any unsure, pre-teen girl would, with a nervous giggle, and a hasty, uncomfortable and self-conscious walk away.

The State Fair was always held in Blackfoot, Idaho, a little old potato producing town, located with the ever-present Union Pacific railroad tracks on the east side and surrounded by farm fields in every other direction. It was about 25 miles from Pocatello and one had to pass through the Bannock Shoshone Indian Reservation located in Fort Hall, to get there. The reservation was depressing, with destitute government built houses and storefronts with bars on the doors and windows. Stray dogs wandered the streets in search of scraps and tumbleweeds blew across the dusty highway. Fort Hall was not a welcoming place. They did however have the only indoor riding facility close to Pocatello. In the bitter cold winter months, it was frequently occupied by many die-hard horse trainers, riders and calf ropers. As the years trudged by, the unfortunate residents of Fort Hall slowly changed their stars. Fort Hall now boasts a luxurious hotel and casino. It is now not only a place where the people of Pocatello can enjoy mild gambling, bingo games and great concerts, but a hospitable destination to western travelers, as well.

One year I qualified for the State Fair in the horse events with Summertime and in the Obedience Class with my dog, Cindy. Not knowing the exact time schedule, we took both my equine and canine partners, just in case I could participate in both classes. As it turned out, the class times overlapped, so I had to make a difficult choice. Surprisingly, even to me, I chose to show Cindy. As I mentioned earlier, Cindy was a mutt, part Brittany Spaniel and part Gordon Setter. She was black with tan paws and muzzle. Many of my dog show friends had expensive registered dogs. The "in" breed seemed to be Irish Setters. With their shiny red coats flowing, they really were stunning dogs. After diligent shampooing, conditioning and brushing of her lovely wavy black coat, Cindy looked just as pretty. She was beautiful in her own way and she was an excellent obedience dog. The one problem I had to deal with was that my parents could not watch us show. If Cindy knew they were around, she would be so preoccupied with finding them in the crowd that she wouldn't pay attention to me. So, I made the long, hot, lonely walk across the fairgrounds infield, from the horse show arena in front of the grandstands to the barn where the dog show was being held, by myself--just a girl and her dog. Since she didn't think my folks were anywhere to be seen, Cindy was flawless, and we won first place. We were Grand Champions of the Eastern Idaho State Fair in the advanced obedience class and received a giant blue and gold rosette ribbon for our efforts. My little mutt out-shined all of those fancy registered dogs. My parents did make it over for the awards ceremony and were so proud of both of us. Their beaming smiles matched mine and Cindy's! She knew she had done well and pranced and wiggled with pride and delight as everyone told her what a good girl she was.

I was really glad I decided to show Cindy that day. I think part of the reason I made that decision, was because of what had happened the year before. I had qualified for showmanship with Summertime but there were so many kids and it was so hot that I passed out in the arena before it was even my turn to show. I remember leaning on Summertime and seeing my mom having conniptions in the stands, waving frantically and gesturing for me to stand up straight and pay attention to the judge. She only wanted me to do well, as all parents do when their children compete, whether in 4-H horse shows or little league baseball. When I finally lost it and slid down Summertime's side and collapsed in a heap in the dry, dusty arena dirt, Rod, who was with Mom and Marilyn watching Paul and I in the horse show hurriedly came down from the grandstand bleachers and took Summertime for me. I think Mom felt bad that she hadn't realized I was in distress. I showed to the judge outside of the arena after the class. I had regained my composure and gotten a much needed drink and relief in the shade. She gave me a disappointing silver ribbon.

It was always great to make it to the State Fair, but once you got there, it was kind of miserable; too hot, too dusty and too many kids and horses.

It was kind of like running for student body vice president to see if you were popular enough to get the most votes and then being so relieved when you lost by two votes so you didn't have to do the job...I'm not divulging anything here, just giving a comparison.

It was nice to be acknowledged, but ...

Chapter 7

I learned many, many lessons while growing up around horses. One of the fairly painful ones, for Summer and me, was that galloping down the side of a paved road is never a good idea. I was coming home from 4-H one day, and was almost back to the farm. I was really tired and thirsty, so, I decided to canter along the side of the road. Something must have startled Summertime, because before I realized what had happened, she'd shied into the road and done a Bambi. A Bambi is something that happens when all four legs slide out from under a critter in different directions. (Remember Bambi on the frozen lake?) Summer was painfully skinned up, with road rash burns on her stifles and knees, where she initially slid and then struggled to regain her feet. Steel shoes on hot pavement are not a good combination. My ego was more injured than my body. I was so ashamed for putting Summertime in a situation to get hurt. I felt bad for a long time and hung my head as I mumbled an explanation of what had happened. But, as I've said before, lesson learned and learned well.

Somewhere along the way Summertime started running away. In other words, she'd start running and I couldn't stop her, no matter how hard I pulled! My Grandpa Gutzman was visiting from Salmon at the time this bad behavior started, so he took me to the local tack store to find a tougher bit. We ended up buying what is called a mechanical hackamore...it sounds worse than it is. This bit doesn't have a mouthpiece, but instead is made up of a leather noseband and a curb chain that fits under the horse's jaw. The action of the noseband and chain clamping together had the desired effect on Summer and she stopped running away with me. Through the years, as my horsemanship continued to improve, I realized that finesse, rather than brute force and a strong, harsh bit, was the answer to most problems of this sort. A simple one rein stop with a rope halter or mild snaffle bit was usually all that was needed for an over anxious horse. I still have that mechanical hackamore and use it every once in a while. My horses love it, now that I have the experienced hands to correctly handle it.

My Grandpa Gutzman was the ultimate horseman. He'd always used horses just for work, not for fun and recreation like I did. He knew how they should be built for optimum performance and what to look for in their conformation. One time, when I was looking for a horse to replace Summertime (I was about to outgrow her) he took me horse shopping. He had a turquoise Dodge truck he called Old George. We spent the day driving on country roads looking for different places that had advertised that they had a horse for sale. I don't think he stopped at one stop sign all day! We didn't find a horse that day but it was still exciting and fun. I loved spending time with Grandpa.

One summer, my cousin and I stayed with Grandpa in Salmon for a week. He catered to us the whole time. Neither of us had our driver's license yet, but we wanted to drive anyway. I was 12 and she was

13. He took us out in the sagebrush covered hills and let us take turns driving Old George. George was a 1969 Dodge short-box pickup with no power steering and, as Grandpa put it "A hard shifting S.O.B." We bounced through the sagebrush, hitting our heads on every bump and grinding gears with every shift; laughing and giggling the whole time.

Grandpa filled the roles of both grandparents to us after my grandma died in 1968, at the very young age of 56. One of my most shameful memories happened one Christmas when she was still alive. She had sewn and knitted an entire wardrobe for a Barbie doll that my parent's had given me. In a spoiled fit, I threw down the Barbie and the little pink suitcase full of tediously made clothes and proclaimed "I hate dolls!" I guess no one had figured that fact all the way out yet. My mother sternly chastised me and told me my Grandma deserved a sincere apology. I sulked back into the festively decorated living room and quietly muttered, "I'm sorry, Grandma, I'll play with the doll and clothes." She simply hugged me and told me it was okay, I was always her favorite, although I don't know why, I was kind of a pill. (I'm sure my brother and cousins would tell you that they were each her favorite too.)

Grandpa would wait for us to arrive for a weekend visit, usually late on a Friday night. There would always be a roast in the oven with mashed potatoes and gravy and a vegetable on the stove. The table was always set for us. During our visits, his entire attention was ours.

He was a selfless, thoughtful man. I was so very lucky to call him Grandpa.

I've heard that girls oftentimes marry a man just like their fathers. I think this was true with my mom. Grandpa was a quiet and gentle man, always generous with his time, talents and love, just like my dad. Although, one difference I recall was that Grandpa had quite a colorful vocabulary.

Once in a while, Grandpa would go to the horse races with my mom and me. He'd stand at the paddock fence and look at the horses. He always looked for a short back and short cannon bone, a good overreach and evidently something else I wasn't aware of, because he could pick winners all day. Now, when I go to the races I try to look for those same things, but I must be leaving something out. I don't hit nearly as many winners as he did. I'm still trying to hone my horse sense skills to the high level possessed by my Grandfather.

*** 1995 ***

Race had such a kind, deep, soulful expression in his beautiful, bright eyes. He always made me feel that he understood every emotion I was feeling down to my core.

No matter how many times I went to the barn or pasture each day, my greeting of "Hi, Racy Roo" was met with his low "huh, huh, huh" nicker, every time, unconditionally.

Race in 1995 as a two-year-old
Always there to greet me, even as a youngster

******

Chapter 8

By 1971, it had become evident to my parents that I was *not* going to outgrow my horse obsession. So, rather than continue to live in town and keep my horse out at the Price farm, they decided to buy an acre in the country and have a house built. If I was going to take care of my own horse, she needed to live with us. My dad fenced the property and he also built a three-sided barn for the horses. I like to think I helped.

I was starting to feel like an authentic, genuine and bona-fide horse person.

Sometime in 1973, my parents had a two-horse custom trailer built. There was a man that lived just around the corner from the Price farm. He and his son had their own little manufacturing business that they operated out of their garage. I remember sitting at their kitchen table and making decisions on just what we wanted in a horse trailer. We decided on a single axle rather than a double, even though the latter is a little more stable in case of a tire blowout. A single axle allowed enough room for a full-length escape door. On double-axle trailers, the escape door is only half size, so you end up having to awkwardly crawl out of it after you load your horse. With the full door, you could simply step out. Since my folks weren't experienced horse people, they wanted it to be as easy as possible for them to help me.

My mom and dad were very thrifty. We never seemed to lack for much, but they took care not to waste either. Since Chad had a workshop with a welding and painting bay, Dad decided he could paint the trailer himself, using Chad's compressor. Dad was so handy that no one ever doubted that he could do anything he tried, even paint a horse trailer. Dad had a pretty blue 1972 Ford pickup that he'd purchased the year before. He painted the horse trailer to match and it was really a nice looking rig when he was all finished, of course he did an excellent job. Every time we drove up to a practice or event in our nice truck and new matching horse trailer, my feelings were pure gratification and happiness.

By the time I was 12, I was starting to outgrow Summertime. Chad had a friend who wanted to buy her and we sold her for $350.00, a very good price for a pony back in the 1970s. It was really hard to sell Summertime. She'd been a great little horse, and she gave me a wonderful start in 4-H. I was fairly tall at about 5'-6" and I just couldn't continue with her. She was only about 13.2 hands or 54 inches at the withers, big for a pony, but small for a horse.

Because I was so tall, I tended to slump my shoulders to try to be less visible and intrusive. I was taller than most of the boys my age, which just added to my feeling of being awkward and clumsy. Unfortunately, that self-imposed bad posture has been a hard habit to break. First my mom and now my husband are forever reminding me to stand up straight.

There was one place I never felt inept or graceless; that was on the back of horse. I may not have been able to run fast or jump high like my brother, but I could ride a horse, while they ran fast and jumped high, so I lived vicariously through my horses, athletically speaking, anyway.

Atop their backs, I sat up tall with confidence.

Sally-1973

Chapter 9

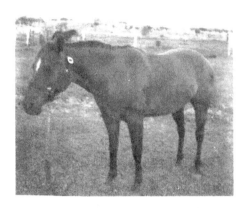

Sally, she was such a pretty horse,
I wish I had a better picture

Since I was quickly becoming too tall for Summertime I started looking for a new horse. I found a 5-year-old, registered Quarter Horse mare for sale with a two-month-old foal by her side. I bought both of them for $200.00. Her registered name was Sally Urturn and I named the foal Brandey.

Sally was bright copper penny sorrel with a white star on her forehead. She was a pretty horse and built just like a Quarter Horse should be. I was so excited to tell the Prices that I finally had a registered Quarter Horse. I soon found out though, that registration papers are not a sure indicator of a good horse. Sally had been used or I should say misused by her previous owners. All she had ever known was that every time she was ridden, she was run until she was exhausted or the children riding her lost interest and put her away, tired and sweaty. She learned from their habits to conserve her energy as much as possible for the next occasion that she would again be run into the ground. Even as a pregnant mare and then a momma nursing a foal, she was ridden too aggressively and always to exhaustion.

Since she had not been well trained or properly handled, I spent countless hours trying to get her ready for the 4-H season. I thought she was just lazy when I first started riding her, but as I thought about the conditions and circumstance that I had witnessed when I bought her, I started to figure out that her past caused her motivation for self-preservation, she needed to maintain herself to be able to effectively feed and care for her foal. I came to the conclusion that, even though she was only five years old, she was just worn out.

Somehow, I made it to the State Fair with Sally in Western Equitation, but we didn't do well. Every time we would pass by the entry gate, she would stop and try to get out. I was so frustrated. I'd spent all summer retraining her and now, at the most important time she was blowing it. I think I ended up with a white ribbon and was devastated. The sour icing on the bitter cake was the judge telling me that I should spend more time riding and training my horse. He told me it was obvious I wasn't committed to doing well or I would've put in more time. I still remember walking down the racetrack at the end of the arena, crying with frustration.

On the up side, Sally was an awesome showmanship horse. She wasn't supposed to move around much; she just needed to walk, trot and then stand squared up and look attentive. She was great at that. With her, I won my first trophy, which, at the time, was one of my greatest goals in life. My brother had all kinds of trophies, from track meets and sports teams, but I'd never won one and I wanted that first trophy, oh, so much.

I remembered watching one of the older boys in my 4-H club win the showmanship class the year before. He stared at the judge the entire class, never taking his eyes off of him, but also keeping his horse standing square and quiet. I actually thought it was kind of weird looking, but his mother commented, "That's what it takes to win at showmanship." So the next year, I was bound and determined to keep my eyes on that judge and "Voila!" It worked. I won my trophy.

Showmanship is one of those classes that doesn't end with the completion of your own class. Since I'd won the horse showmanship class, I had to compete in what is called a Round Robin. This is a class where the winners of all of the other showmanship classes compete with each other's animals. My show experience was limited to dogs and horses, but now I had to show a sheep, a goat, a pig, and a cow. The cow was a Holstein milk cow and she was taller than my horse. I was petrified. Also, I was clueless; the only animal I showed correctly was the goat, because you show them similarly to the way you show dogs. With the pig, you only get to use a stick to herd it. I was a bad pig herder and I couldn't get the sheep to move. I was never so glad to have a class be over, and I absolutely didn't care that I didn't win; it was just a huge relief to get back my well-behaved horse. In subsequent years, since my first trophy had been attained, I always did well enough in showmanship to get a gold ribbon, but not the best, no more giant cows and stubborn sheep for me.

Of course, I made it to State Fair in showmanship that year. Unfortunately, this time I messed up big time. There was a judge at one end of the arena and a ring steward at the other. The ring steward was carrying a clipboard and making notes. The judge didn't have anything to write on. I figured the guy with the clipboard was the judge, so you guessed it; I looked at the ring steward the entire class. No trophy this time. Oh well, at least there was no terrifying State Fair Round Robin to contend with.

After the State Fair and the judge's unfounded remarks, I decided it was time to sell Sally and get to training on Brandey. A heavyset girl and her parents came to look at Sally to buy her. I had her grazing in the neighbor's pasture when they arrived, so I just ran over with a halter and lead rope, caught her, jumped on and rode her back to our house. That was just about all it took to sell her to these people. They saw how gentle she was and she really was very pretty. I asked if the girl wanted to ride her, but she said no, and just continued to stroke Sally on the neck. I think she just wanted a horse for a pet.

I sold Sally for $350.00 and still had Brandey. Pretty savvy business move, eh? I used part of the money to buy myself hard contact lenses. I hated being blind but I wouldn't wear my glasses--too geeky. As it ended up, I couldn't wear the contacts either. I remember wearing them to school for the first time, I was sitting in an 8th grade English class, with tears streaming down my face and nonstop sniffing of my runny nose. The teacher asked if I was all right, I said "Yeah, I just have new contacts." I guess you were eventually supposed to build up little calluses on the inside of your eyelids so the contacts wouldn't seem so abrasive. I couldn't ever stand to have them in long enough to build up those calluses, so, I finally had to give in and start wearing my ostracizing glasses. I hated having to wear glasses. I believed it was one of the great injustices of the world. Technology would improve and later in my life I would be free from near-sightedness, but not soon enough to save me from having to wear glasses through the rest of junior high and high school.

I loathed junior high. I always thought everyone was just looking at me and thinking, "That is one un-cool girl." I had a couple of good friends, but for the most part, I just endured 7th, 8th and 9th grades. However, when I left that school building and went home to my horse, I immediately felt better. It was a feeling of well-being, I felt lighter and happier. I was still kind of awkward and introverted, but I was working on it.

Brandey was going to be a big part of my transformation.

*** *2006* ***

When Race was gone so suddenly, I felt as if I lost who I was. He had been part of my everyday life and part of me, for the last thirteen years. It seemed like I couldn't go on being me without him.

The realization that I would never be able to sit on his beautiful back and feel his immense strength, his gentle way of moving and that extraordinary closeness ever again, was more than I could handle.

I could feel the cold fingers of depression taking hold of me and I couldn't seem to do anything to stop them....

******

Chapter 10

Brandey and Susan in 1975

Brandey was seal bay, almost black with a hint of light brown with a black mane and tail. He had some tiny specks of white on his hips. His sire was an Appaloosa. Since he didn't look like the typical Appy, I always had a hard time convincing people he was. Other than spots, though, there are several other characteristics of the Appaloosa breed and Brandey had all of them. His lips were mottled, his hooves were striped and the whites around his eyes were visible most of the time.

I'd had Brandey since he was two months old and we were very much in tune with each other. My parents bought me a book that would help me train Brandey. Understanding and Training Horses by James Ricci was the beginning of my horse-training journey. I read and re-read that book until I was familiar with every concept on every page. I made notes in the margins and highlighted parts that I knew I would want to refer back to often. The author started from the very beginning, with a horse's natural reactions and tendencies. I believe this author and horseman was one of the first great naturals, and I am so glad that I was exposed to the natural way of doing things with horses. Because of that book, I feel I started out right with my attitude and philosophies toward horse training. Later when the new natural horsemanship movement began in the 1990s, I was happy to realize that I'd already been using many of the gentler techniques and methods.

As a horse crazy girl, with a 2-year-old colt as my only horse, I spent every spare moment with him. I'd started his training with groundwork when he was still a foal. Getting him to move away from the pressure of my hands on his sides and shoulders, he quickly learned to be very light in his movements. When it was time to ride him for the first time, he seemed to be already broke. Much to my parent's dismay, that first ride occurred while I was home alone. I had Brandey tied to the side of the horse trailer, I put on the bareback pad and I got on. No big deal. As I rode him more and more, we became so in harmony with each other, I rarely used a bridle or halter, most of the time when I was riding in the pasture, I just had a thin rope around his neck.

We practiced running barrels in the pasture. With just one slight nudge with my inside heel he would bend around the barrel. I quickly learned that I had to move with him, as one, to stay balanced and centered because he was so quick and agile.

He was such a joy to ride and very willing to try most anything I wanted. One day I decided to ride him along the canal and then down the road to a house where I mowed the lawn for an elderly couple that raised sheep. He was fine all the way over. He didn't mind the water or the traffic, but wasn't sure he had any real reason to like the sheep. I put him in a small pasture next to some of the smelly, wooly critters while I mowed the lawn. He paced and carried on the entire time I was mowing. By the time I was finished and ready to head home, he looked like he had just finished a 25-mile endurance race. Even though he was tired from his exhaustive tantrum in the sheep pasture, Brandey safely carried me home. I don't think he held a grudge, but on our return ride, I got an ear full, telepathically of course, that he would prefer that I *not* park him next to the woolies ever again! He never did become comfortable with smaller creatures; even ponies pulling a cart could pretty much send him to the moon.

Since I'd sold Sally, Brandey was my new 4-H horse. I think I was only in 4-H with Brandey for one year before I moved onto high school rodeo and other interests. I spent every waking minute with him and we had a really good time that last year.

In our backyard, we had a small, square pasture. I used this area to work on gaits and cues. Since it was small, Brandey developed a lovely little trot that anybody could sit. He also had a nice slow lope, just what the judges liked to see in Western Pleasure and Equitation classes. Also, probably a remnant from my younger days on Star, I still rode without a saddle a lot and Brandey's easy gaits made riding bareback a true pleasure. Look out bareback dollar class!

Brandey was only three at this time, quite young for a 4-H horse, but you use what you have, and what I had was a gem. I recall one class in particular, Western Equitation; we had a great class, no mistakes, perfect leads, easy transitions, and an excellent back up. We were standing in line while the judge and steward discussed the class placings. I knew it was between a friend of mine from another club and me. They stood behind us and discussed the class. The anticipation was excruciating and almost unbearable. We waited and waited as it seemed like it was taking them forever. They finally made a decision and the announcer called, "First place goes to number 9, Susan Deagle." My mom whooped from the stands and I was so excited that Brandey and I almost ran over the ribbon girl. Needless to say, Brandey was such a remarkable horse that this was just the first of many times his number would be

called, whether with me, or with my children. Some of
those stories will come later.

After that year in 4-H, I moved on and started
riding in a ladies riding club called the Silver Sage Riders.
Since I was only 15, I needed someone that was already
in the club to sponsor me. I had a friend who lived just
a few houses down the road from us. She and her mother
and sisters all rode in the club. She said her oldest sister
would sponsor me, if I wanted to ride. It sounded fun, so
I asked my folks and they seemed to think it would be a
good thing to be involved with. I was still too young to
drive at night, so one of them had to take me to the
fairgrounds two nights a week for practice. Mom always
enjoyed watching me with the horses, so I don't think she
minded too much. The riding club was a member of the
Idaho Riding Association which included men's, women's
and family groups. We had District and State meets
every summer.

We performed a rehearsed drill as music blared at
full volume over the loudspeakers of the grandstands.
Ghost Riders in the Sky was our theme song. I was the
youngest in the group; most of the ladies were in their
30s and 40s. The drill part of the club was only tolerable
because we did it at a gallop. We also had to do a parade
drill, ugh! I hated that part of the competitions. We had
to walk down the road and do silly crisscrosses, carry
flags and wear matching uniforms. Our outfits were
bright kelly green and white, with white boots and green
hats. For the horses, we had fluffy white saddle pads,

white bridles and white breast collars. The horses actually looked pretty spiffy in all of their white tack.

Brandey and Susan dressed in
Silver Sage Uniform and Tack

That was all fine and well, but the real reason I joined the club was for the games. The team relay games required high speed, high athleticism on the part of horse and rider, with the added pressure of competition. The games included the cloverleaf barrel race and pole bending, which came in handy when I was ready to try high school rodeo.

Another game I loved was the scurry race. A team of three riders jumped their horses over three jumps then turned around a barrel, rode back over the jumps and handed off a baton to the next team member. The competition was fast and furious. We had two additional teammates that ran along the outside of the jumps to reset the pole if one our horses knocked one down. Before the next rider could go, the poles all had to be reset. The baton pass was always a vital part of the race. The waiting horses were flighty with anticipation as the other horses on the team ran the course, so sometimes just getting the horses to face the right direction so we could reach the baton was a challenge. No matter the outcome, we always had fun fun fun!

Brandey and Susan running the Scurry Race

There were also flag races, figure eight races, a potato race of course, after all we *were* in Idaho, plus a rescue race, trailer race and flat track relay.

My first year, as the youngest (dumbest?), I even volunteered to be on the wild cow milking team. So insanely crazy!   We were competing against men's groups, so the strength thing (or lack thereof) really came into play with this one.

A halter with a long lead rope was somehow put on a wild cow. Then three young women were expected to power it to a stop and milk it! Really?! Picture this: six wild cows, running madly around the arena, dragging men and women on the ends of the lead ropes. We were just glad to get out of the arena with our heads intact. We suffered plenty of rope burns, but we survived and vowed *never* to do that again, we agreed that we would concede that dangerous game to the men next year.

The speed games though--those were the ones for me! Since I was raised with the Price boys who were all destined to be jockeys, the thrill of racing around the oval track had always appealed to me. I knew I could never be a jockey, too tall and not thin enough, so this was my only chance to ride in a race on the track. It was the mile relay and each of four horse and rider teams ran a quarter mile leg. Brandey wasn't the race horse type, but a friend in the club had an ex-race horse named Dooby. She was more than a little hesitant to ride in the relay, so Dooby was all mine for the big race.

We practiced a couple of times on the track at the Bannock County Fairgrounds. Dooby and I were the anchor leg of our team, since he was the only horse in the club that had actually raced.   The air was electric with anticipation as those of us running the anchor leg of the relay, waited and watched as the other riders each raced around their quarter of the track and then handed the baton to the next team member. We had a blast in the practice races and oh, what a thrill! But, when it came time for the real race, our first two riders dropped the baton, so Dooby and I never got to run our leg. It took me a while to realize my team was not coming around the track, dammit! I was so bummed, oh, well, at least we got to run in the practice races and I was able to know the thrill and exhilaration of running full throttle on a big, strong, powerful racehorse.

Brandey had a few idiosyncrasies and one of them was his reaction to electric clippers. Most Appaloosas have thin, scraggly manes and tails. His, on the other hand, were full and nice, I guess since he was only *half* Appy. The problem was I could never get his thick mane to lie over nicely on his neck. He had a lovely neck so I decided to just roach his mane instead of constantly fighting it to get it to lie over. A roached mane is simply shaved off. I would always leave a little bit of hair at the base of his neck. That patch of mane was needed on his wither so I could hang on to it and swing up on him when I rode bareback. For a few years, I cut it with scissors, which was a huge job and took a lot of time and patience for an entire mane, and it was nearly impossible to get it to look really neat and trim. We'd sometimes borrow other people's clippers to roach him, but that was difficult because he needed to be restrained, just a bit, to behave like a good boy. By restrained, I don't mean tied down tight, something as simple as a lead rope around his body was enough. As long as he couldn't move around and fuss, he was fine. However, if he wasn't snug against something he would dance away and lift his head high in the air. He would become so agitated and worked up that I couldn't even get close to him with the noisy electric clippers. I finally got my own set of clippers as a birthday present so I was able to work with Brandey to desensitize him to them. This helped and he did start to accept and tolerate the clippers more and more with each lesson. Even so, I realized the best way to clip his mane was to make him feel secure and he would stay calm and cool and get a great looking haircut.

We discovered this while dealing with another little problem that arose with Brandey when I was in high school and riding with the Silver Sage Riders. The club had just upgraded to new matching blankets. They were horsehair on the underneath side with a border of a green and white pattern on the top. The blanket must have had an odd smell to Brandey. My truck and trailer were all hooked up and I was getting ready to haul to a rodeo where the club was performing. This was an especially fun, small town rodeo as there were carnival rides and games, a parade and other festivities; we were all looking forward to our performance. Brandey was tied to the horse trailer and just as I started to swing the new blanket on him, he got a whiff of the horsehair and for some reason it totally freaked him out.

I don't know if he thought I was trying to throw a dead horse on him or what, but in a flash, his eyes got huge, he snorted and cow kicked me right in the pelvis. My mom said all she heard from the house was "Oh my god!" "Thwack" The kick sent me flying and my ten feet of air travel landed me painfully on the hard graveled ground. Brandey was snorting and blowing and shaking all over, he was absolutely petrified of the new blanket. Mom came running out to find me lying in the gravel parking area next to the horse and trailer. She moved me to the house and onto the couch and I asked her to call someone in the club and tell them we wouldn't be making it to the rodeo. Then we were off to the hospital emergency room to find out the extent of the damage. Once we got there, the nurses got me out of the car and onto a stretcher. They really scared Mom by telling her she never should have moved me, because a broken bone could have punctured my bladder or some other organ. She was upset enough without someone telling her that she'd put her only daughter at risk. They took the x-rays and determined that nothing was broken, but my pelvis bone had been shifted, it now looked like a chunky zipper that was not correctly lined up. The doctor didn't know what kind of problem that misalignment might cause if I ever had a baby. Guess we would just have to wait and see. They put me on crutches since it was excruciating for me to move my legs one at a time. With the crutches, I could swing both legs together and crutch along at a pretty good pace.

In the meantime, while I was healing, we still needed to get Brandey used to that new, scary blanket. We called Chad and he said to bring him over and we could put him in their doctoring chute and slowly introduce the blanket to him. So, Mom and Dad loaded him in the trailer with me giving instructions from the sidelines on my crutches. We got to the farm and Chad took over. Eventually, Brandey accepted the blanket and let Chad put it on him. The restriction of the chute allowed Brandey to actually think about the blanket before he panicked over it. That was when we figured out that a little bit of restraint really helped Brandey cope with things that frightened him.

As we were getting ready to load up and go home, Brandey decided he was not going to get back in the trailer. That lovely, nearly-new horse trailer, how dare he?! Before, he had always been a *hit or miss* kind of loader. If the mood struck him just right he would hop right in, sometimes he needed just a little encouragement and then other times, like that evening, he refused. This was a major error in judgment on Brandey's part. Chad had raised and trained horses all of his life and his patience with insolent Appaloosas was not long. After a couple of refusals to get in the trailer, Chad wound up and booted Brandey a good one in the gut. That got his attention, but still he would not load up. I'd always babied him and led him in and then I would step out the escape door. Anytime one of my horses acted a little spoiled, Chad would say "Well, now, it looks like that horse has been Susanized!" Not many names get turned into verbs, I kind of liked it!

No babying from Chad. Not only was Brandey to get in, he was to get in on his own, without having to be led. So, one more swift boot to the belly with the rope thrown up over his neck and he jumped in that trailer like it was the best idea ever! That was all it took to perfect Brandey's trailer loading. From that night on, all that was necessary was to open the gate, throw the rope over his neck and ask him to jump in. In my later years, this was not the approach I took with trailer loading training, but it worked with Brandey. I was forever grateful for the evening of lessons that my *Susanized* horse received from Chad that night.

I remained in Silver Sage for several more years. As soon as I turned 16 and could drive at night, my parents were only too happy to turn over the truck and trailer to me. They would watch from our back deck to see when the arena lights went out up at the fairgrounds, and then give me about half an hour to make it home before they started to worry. If I didn't show up, they would drive to the fairgrounds, which was only about three miles up the road, to make sure we were okay and safely on our way home.

They would usually find me chatting with friends and neglecting to realize that the lights had been turned off and the clock was ticking for my return. Sometimes this would irritate me, but I guess I should have appreciated the fact that they were just being good guardians. Later in life, as my own children were occasionally late for curfews, I understood.

Chapter 11

During junior high and then again in high school, I was basically known as Dan Deagle's little sister. This meant I was tolerated by the junior and senior athletes and popular guys at Highland High School, but just barely. I wasn't part of the "in" crowd like Dan was. I wasn't in drill team or a cheerleader. I couldn't even do a cartwheel, although the summer before my sophomore year in my quest to break in to the well-liked clique, I took a dance and cheer class. I learned to do the splits, but I never could master the ever elusive cartwheel. I was so disappointed when I tried out for the Highland Scotties, the sophomore flag team, as I was all set to show off that I could now do the splits; then they weren't even called for in the routine. All I was supposed to do was march in time with the music, Ha! easier said than done, I didn't make the team. Unfortunately, there was no rhythm in my bones whatsoever. In later years my husband would laugh when I'd try to clap along with the band at our son's football games. I did finally discover that there was *some* rhythm in there; it just took a couple of cocktails to allow it to escape. It seemed all of a sudden, I miraculously had rhythm. I'm sure the other spectators or in some cases dance floor occupants probably didn't hear the same beat that I was feeling, but at that point I didn't care. It was my beat and I was sticking to it!

My sophomore year, I had two good friends and we basically existed in the not-so-cool world of high school.

We did join pep club, at least we could cheer our team on, just not with any sort of coordination.

Just as my sophomore year was winding down, my brother's girlfriend, Stacey, suggested that I should like James, her next door neighbor and her brother's best friend. He was my age and I knew who he was and thought he was cute. She somehow put a bug in James' ear that he should ask me out and he did. We went to the drive-in movie and as he held my hand, I felt a startling new sensation. My stomach was doing flip flops. At the end of the night he dropped me off and as I went inside I said looking back over my shoulder "Call me?" and he said he would.

The next day, his sister was getting married so he didn't have time to call. Of course, with my low self-esteem, I just assumed one date was enough for him to realize that I was not cheerleader caliber and would *not* be a wise choice for a girlfriend. I moped around my bedroom all day waiting for the phone to ring. Later that night, after all of the wedding festivities had ended, and the newlyweds had been sent on their way, Stacey came over with a bouquet from the wedding and a message from James that he was sorry he hadn't called. He called the next day and we started dating. We were pretty much inseparable all through our junior and senior years. I let my friendships take a backseat to my relationship with James and I have always regretted that. But now, instead of being known as Dan's little sister, I had a new title, I was James' girlfriend. Someday, I hoped to have my own identity, but for now, it was just a relief to be in the right crowd through the rest of high school.

James was not crazy about horses, but he was crazy about me, so he tried to like Brandey. One night after Silver Sage practice, he came up to the fairgrounds to say Hi. Brandey rubbed his bridle on his car and he was mad for a week. I don't even think it was scratched, but the clunk of the steel bit on his shiny new dark blue Ford Pinto sounded like it was something he should be upset over.

James was very serious about our relationship and started talking like we should get married; we even had a name picked out for a baby boy. We were going to call him Christofer James; it was just young love talking. James and I eventually broke up after high school. I felt we should at least date some other people before we started seriously talking marriage. I was only 17 and he was really the only steady boyfriend I'd ever had.

After our first year in college, we tried it again. But, we had grown into different people and we just didn't click anymore. I know I broke his heart, but as fate would have it, we both ended up marrying wonderful people and our lives somewhat paralleled each other's. We each married someone who had been married before with a child from their first marriage, then we each had two boys. Our first son, TJ and his first son, John, were born just a week apart. We kept track of each other and our families through our parents and siblings.

And then, when TJ and John were just 9 years old, the unimaginable happened. James died... at the much too young age of 30.....he died from cancer that started with a Melanoma mole on his temple. I felt guilty... it seemed that I should have been his widow, that, had I married him, his wife and children wouldn't be going through this heartbreaking time. I will always be grateful to his wife; she was so warm and gracious at his memorial and she allowed me to grieve for James, too.

At the graveside service, I gave James' #5 Highland Rams football jersey to his young son, John.

Years later, when TJ was moving into his dorm room at Boise State, there were four names on the door; Tony and John, Nick and TJ. The dorm room was a quad with two beds on each side of a center wall and a shared bathroom and shower at the front. We didn't get to meet any of TJ's roommates the day we moved him in, but figured we'd have a chance to get to know them on a future visit. About three days after TJ moved in, he called me and said "Guess who one of my roommates is?" I had no guess. He went on "James' son, John." Oh...my...gosh! Of all of the dorm rooms in the country, or even just at Boise State University, what are the chances of TJ and John, these two boys who had never met, but whose lives had already been on a fairly parallel path, being randomly placed in the same room? This was just amazing and unbelievable to me.

After telling my husband of this tremendous coincidence, I immediately called James' mother, Marie, to tell her of this Karmic event. She, too, found it remarkable. Marie remained one of my most cherished friends. She was full of life and light, even though she had lost two children and her husband. She was tiny in stature but mighty in heart.

On our next visit, John answered the dorm room door when I knocked; his eyes lit up, he smiled, shook my hand and said "I remember you. You gave me my dad's jersey at the cemetery." What a wonderful feeling. TJ and John remain friends today; and that makes me smile.

Chapter 12

Many great things came out of the Silver Sage experience, not only the friendships and all of the horse fun, but Brandey became skilled at speed events. He was much too young to be running such hard and physically challenging events, but I didn't know that at the time. He was the only horse I had, so I used him for everything.

Over his three and four-year-old years, he bowed a tendon and suffered splints in his front legs. I treated the injuries and allowed him to heal. I now know that a colt's knees and legs are not fully developed until they are at least five years old.

Brandey was so young when I started high school that I only participated in rodeo with him my senior year, when he was five. The barrel racing and pole bending that we did in Silver Sage were also high school rodeo events, so he already had his training to jump right in to rodeo as soon as I felt he was mature enough to hold up to the rigors of competition.

Remember those stupid glasses that I had to wear all through high school? Well, at my first high school rodeo, those damn glasses really got in the way. In my first run, after I turned the first barrel and looked up to the second barrel, my glasses fell down to my nose. I had to push them back up and try to get on line to the second barrel all at the same time. Needless to say, we did not have a good first run. I was so disgusted I decided not to wear my glasses for my second run. Funny thing about not being able to see, your balance is a little out of whack, so running barrels blind didn't work very well either. My depth perception was also affected, so, the timing of my cues to Brandey was off, so I had a second unsatisfactory run.

My memories of running Brandey on poles are so intense and vivid that I can almost feel the excitement and thrill of his fast, smooth runs all over again. As long as I stayed out of his way, and let him go, he was smooth as silk. He wasn't as fast and powerful as some of the other horses that were, for the most part Quarter Horses; many of them, ex-racehorses with huge rear ends to drive them around the poles and barrels and then accelerate at breakneck speeds. Brandey made up for his lack of great speed with his remarkable consistency. He rarely, if ever hit a pole or barrel. When the events are made up of two or three go rounds, consistency is key.

We were always competitive in barrels but not usually at the top of the leader board. But in pole bending, we were tough. I remember the District Rodeo. The first day was beautiful and sunny, the arena was well worked and fast with good footing. After our first run in poles, we were sitting sixth in the standings. You had to be in the top four to make it to the State Finals, so I felt I had a real shot this year. We only had two runs to net our average, so my second run had to be fast and clean. Well, the rodeo stars were not shining brightly on us the next day. The first half of the second go was run in the morning; the sun was still shining and the arena still good. The second half of the second go was in the evening. It had started raining in the early afternoon and by evening the arena looked like mud soup. Those of us who had the misfortune of drawing into that section of the go round, knew there was no way to have a fast time in that arena. We were all just happy to finish our runs and have our horses still healthy. It would have been so easy for them to be injured running and turning, fast and tight, in the sloppy and slick mud. But that was just the luck of the draw and the sometimes bitter reality of rodeo. I was obviously disappointed, but what are you going to do? I think I ended up finishing in the top twelve, but that's a long way from the top four. I put Brandey away in his stall and made my way dejectedly through the rain back to the camper that my dad had parked next to the arena. As Mom and I lay up on the over-cab bed and watched the rest of the go round, I empathized with the contestants still enduring the wretched weather.

That was the end of my high school rodeo career; it was fun for that one year. I realized I loved the electric and stimulating atmosphere and wanted to be a part of the rodeo way of life. I also learned more of the nature of rodeo as a sport and those lessons would serve me well in my future competitive endeavors.

I started competing in jackpot rodeos over the summer. A jackpot is usually held at a private arena or county fairgrounds. A group of riders get together and pay an entry fee for the events that they want to participate in. The winners are then paid out of the entry fees. Events included barrel racing, pole bending and goat tying. If calves were available, there would also be breakaway calf roping.

That fall, I started classes at Idaho State University. I was excited because I thought Brandey was a good enough pole bending horse that we could be competitive at the next level. There was a girl in my dorm that was in the ISU Rodeo Club, so I went to the first meeting with her. I sat through the entire meeting and nothing was ever said about pole bending. When I finally asked about it, they told me college rodeo didn't have pole bending as an event. Thus, my college rodeo career ended before it ever began. It never occurred to me to look for another horse that would be competitive in barrels. Some girls pulled in to rodeos with a trailer full of high priced horses; a specialized horse for every event. Not me. Brandey was my one and only horse, if I couldn't use him, I just didn't participate.

So, I continued running at the local jackpot rodeos. I made quite a bit of money with Brandey in pole bending and barrels, and for a few years, I consistently received year-end awards for both events. I still have many of the blankets, bridle-sets, stable sheets, duffle bags, and my favorite, an engraved custom made leather breast collar, proclaiming us high money winners in *Novice Barrels 1988*.

Brandey was so outstanding; I was starting to gain confidence in myself, through my confidence in him.

Chapter 13

I started college in 1978. I was enrolled in the Design Drafting Program at Idaho State University. My first year, I lived in the dorms, even though my folks lived just 20 minutes away. I was awarded a presidential scholarship from the university that paid all of my tuition, fees, books and equipment expenses. Since my parents were always very organized with their finances, my brother and I each had a college fund. Because of the scholarship, I didn't need the money for college, so Mom and Dad said if I wanted to live on campus, they would pay for it. I was 18 and ready to be out on my own. A friend from high school and I decided to be roommates. It was the best of both worlds. I had my independence, but I also had the security of my mom and dad, Kacey, my first German Shorthaired Pointer, Booze, our champagne colored cat, and of course my horse, Brandey, just across town.

I was in a primarily male dominated field of study at the university and most of my classmates were of the testosterone variety. Of course they were. Most of my friends, all of my life, had been boys. There was one other female in the class and she and I became lifelong friends. I dated some of the guys in my class, but it was mostly just going out as friends, no scorching chemistry with any of them, but good guys all the same.

In high school I had been such a prude. I didn't take part in parties or drinking, and absolutely NO drugs! When I started college and was placed in the middle of this class with all of these culturally and economically diverse people, it was quite an eye opener. I gradually started becoming more open minded and more accepting of other people's differences.

As I opened my mind to this new world of diversity, I also started to come out of my shell. The confidence I was gaining from this new set of classmates was incredible. That shy, introverted personality was starting to shift. A more outgoing, fun-loving young woman was finally emerging.

I had been a very judgmental person all of my life. I think it stemmed from being so insecure in myself. Through these new friendships, I discovered that just because someone does something like, say, comes to Physics class stoned, doesn't make them a bad person. This particular event happened quite often in our 1:00 Physics class, lunchtime *study* session anyone? The distractive behavior finally calmed down when the rest of the class insisted that the instructor not go over everything a second (and sometimes a third) time for the affected students. I am happy to say these students made the positive adjustment necessary and buckled down to their studies. We turned out to be an exceptional class of designers and several of my classmates went on to start their own engineering and design firms and had extremely successful careers.

Chapter 14

After starting my second year of college, I realized it was time to spread my wings a little further than my class of 12 and get a real social life started.

There was a sandwich shop right across from the university and sometimes we would land there after a long week of classes. It was there that I learned how to chug beer. The drinking age way back in the days of my youth was 19, so I was legal, of course. I was still a little bit of a prude and unwilling to put myself into a situation that would get me into trouble or disappoint my parents.

After my first semester living in the dorm, I realized that I could still experience college life while living off campus. So, I moved back home at the beginning of my second semester.

I'd met a girl that was a friend of a friend and we hit it off. We decided to go out to the Oxbow Bar one night after playing racquetball earlier in the day. It was indeed a very fateful night; for it was the night I met the love of my life.

We were dancing with different boys as they asked us. One in particular kept asking me, but he was too tall and too drunk and I felt like I had to hold him up. He was just one in the many hordes of Utah students that would come up to Idaho to drink. The legal drinking age in Utah was 21. During the course of the night, a very good looking young man kept looking at our table. I assumed he was looking at my friend, she was cute and petite and nobody ever really looked at me in a crowd. He finally came over and I expected him to ask her to dance but he asked me instead, what a shock! We danced, he was a great dancer. I was not. I was trying desperately not to look like a klutz, because this guy was so remarkable. We danced once and then sat back down at our separate tables. The drunken kid kept monopolizing my time so I finally told him "No more dances!"

I was hoping that the good looking guy would ask me again; if I hadn't blown it the first time with my unfortunate dancing. Miracle! He asked for another dance and when the song ended we sat down together and started talking. He eventually went back to his table and asked the girl he was actually with for a pen to get my name and number. He swears they were just friends, but I always thought it was a bit awkward. Regardless, I'm certainly glad he asked for that pen.

I told him my name...my real name. I sometimes used a fake name at the clubs. Something about this man was different. His name was Rocke. Not Rock-Y, he was quick to point out. He asked if he could call me and I said yes and gave him my number. As we visited, I told him what I was studying in college and that I almost got married, and with that he said "I did." What?! Come to find out, he was not only divorced, but had a two-year-old little girl. Wow, didn't see that one coming. Even with all of this information, I was very intrigued and quite smitten with this young man. He was four years older than I and seemed so worldly.

As my mom tells it, when I got home that night and tip-toed into their bedroom to tell them I was home, she said I leaned up against the wall and said, "I'm in like," (big sigh!) Boy was I! It was pretty much love at first sight.

Chapter 15

The next day, I went with my good friend, Paul, to the chariot races. We had a team together. Of course, they were Price horses, but I got to drive them once in a while with Chad and Paul to exercise them and I was in charge of making them showy on race day. Sir Aaron and Tough To Pass were the racing Quarter Horses on our team.

Sir Aaron was a stallion and they used him for many years as the main stud on the farm. He was a sweet, sweet horse. I remember once, watching Paul's Grandma Gerti feeding him. She just told him to "Get back, Aaron" and he waited patiently at the back of the stall until she finished feeding him. Not until she was completely out of his stall, would he move up to eat. He was jet black with just a tiny white spot on his forehead. Tough was a bay (bright mahogany brown with black mane, tail and lower legs) and he had a striking white blaze on his face. He was also a really nice horse. Our team colors were red and white, so we made lots of pompoms out of bright red and white yarn. We would set up a table in the basement and spend hours making those pompoms and talking about how fantastic our team was going to look on race day. I would braid the horse's manes and tie the pompoms all the way down their necks, then we would french braid their tails and tie a couple on top. They were a very spiffy looking team, and we won the 'Best Groomed Team' award for the Idaho State Chariot Racing Association that year.

Chad offered to let me drive a chariot team out of the starting gates by myself. Of course, it wasn't our big-time team, but a couple of back-up horses. Chad Boy, a flashy white Appy gelding (named after Chad) and a young Thoroughbred were the two horses I was going to drive. This particular day, it had been raining and snowing. Chariot racing in Idaho is a winter sport. The track was muddy, but the plan had been made for me to drive out of the gates that day, so I did. After the last official race of the day, Chad and the boys hitched up Chad Boy and the Thoroughbred and I drove them over to the gates with Casey in the cart with me. He was giving me instructions all the way over. When I got to the starting gate, Rod was there to head the horses. A Header refers to the person who holds onto the horses in the starting gate.

Casey stuck a whip in my mouth, looped the reins through my hands, and showed me where to hang on for "take off." (If you don't hang on tight, you will be thrown out of the back of the chariot when the horses bolt out of the starting gate.) Casey was telling me to whip the Thoroughbred because Chad Boy would burst out of the gates faster than him. Rod was saying, "No, don't tell her to whip, she should just drive." Well, the gates flew open, the horses dug in to the muddy track and we were off. After the initial bolt out of the gates, I flipped the whip towards the Thoroughbred's rump. I don't think I ever made contact. I shifted the reins to both hands and we were flying. Oh, what a thrill. The power and speed of these horses was unbelievable, and they weren't even the fast ones! With the wind and the sleet and the mud hitting me in the face, I was a mess, but I didn't care. I was having so much fun!   As soon as I passed the grandstands, I started pulling to slow down the team; I had them stopped before I reached the backstretch where Marilyn was waiting to help me take the horses back to the barns. As she hopped in the cart behind me, she told me I shouldn't start to pull them to a stop until I'm around the curve. Oh well, maybe next time. Well, there never was a next time; that was my one and only run from the gates.

That year we made it to the World Cutter and Chariot Racing Finals in the second division and ended up fourth at World's. Paul still has a huge trophy to show for our efforts. Our two beautiful horses ran very well, and they looked fantastic!

A few years later, I contemplated driving a team in actual races, but something happens to a woman after she has children. At least it happened to me. I didn't have the nerve any more. Maybe self-preservation mode kicked in because I knew I had children to nurture. I don't know exactly why I didn't want to do it. I do know I will certainly always remember that "flight" down the track, getting covered in mud and having a blast!

When I got home that February afternoon in 1980, my mom said I had a call from a guy "with a soft voice." She said he told her he would call back later. He did. We went out on our first date that night. Wow, he said he would call and he did, the very next day! We went to an Italian restaurant called Gabbertino's in Pocatello. Rocke ordered wine, I have never been much of a wine connoisseur, but that night we had Riunite Lambrusco, and to this day, if I'm going to drink wine; that's the kind I prefer. We had a great time, it was very easy to talk with each other and it didn't have the awkward feel of most first dates. We made plans to go skiing the next day for our second date. I'd never skied in my life, but Rocke said he would teach me and I was so infatuated with him that I was willing to try anything, just to spend more time with this wonderful man.

Rocke and I had a whirlwind romance. We saw each other almost every day. He was so full of life and fun. He always wanted to be doing something. I needed a person like that in my life, as I didn't venture out of my comfort zone very easily. We went on ski trips to Wyoming, fishing and swimming out on the little lakes of southeast Idaho, and he even rode horses with me.

His daughter's name was Jennifer, an absolutely beautiful child with long blonde hair and thick black eyelashes shading bright blue eyes. For her third birthday, we borrowed Chad Boy. We hauled him to Rocke's house in an older part of town for a little birthday party. We invited a couple of little kids from the neighborhood over and gave rides on Chad Boy around the yard. This was Jennifer's first exposure to horses and she was instantly smitten. No fear, she just wanted to ride and ride and ride. I can't remember why we didn't use Brandey, probably because he was a little too nervous and over-sensitive for kiddy rides. But as Jennifer grew up, Brandey would become a huge part of her life.

Rocke and I talked about marriage very early in our courtship. He was a little gun-shy, because his first marriage had failed, so he wanted to just live together. My mom and dad had pretty strong old-fashioned views on the subject of living together before being married. I knew they would have a hard time accepting it if I chose to go that route with my life and as I've mentioned before, I never wanted to disappoint them. I told Rocke, "No, we couldn't live together, but we didn't need to rush into getting married either." I was enjoying dating Rocke and felt very confident that he was "the one." I could wait until he was comfortable with taking the plunge again.

I did decide that since I was in such a serious and committed relationship, it was time for me to move out on my own. I'd only lived in the dorm with my friend for about a semester. The thought of getting an apartment of my own was pretty exciting. I started looking and found a cute little basement apartment on 8th Street, just down from the University where I was finishing up my Design Drafting Program. I gave the landlady a $50 deposit to hold it for me.

I guess something about me moving into a place of my own made Rocke think that maybe he was more ready to get married again than he thought. One night before I moved, Rocke called around 11:30. He was a little "lit up" I guess you could say. He asked if I wanted to get married. I was a little hesitant; of course I wanted to marry him, but I wanted to make sure he remembered asking me, so I told him to ask again tomorrow.

The next day was pure torture and when we finally saw each other that night, Rocke claimed he didn't have anything to ask me. He was just teasing and asked in a more proper way. I still didn't get the 'down on one knee with ring in hand' proposal, but a very sincere and special one all the same.

We went ring shopping together, which I am thankful for because I absolutely loved our rings. My engagement ring was a tiny little diamond on a bright gold band with crisscrosses etched around it and our wedding bands matched. I thought they were perfect, just like my man. I think we spent $400 total on all three rings and that was probably really more than we could afford. I see the huge diamonds that girls are getting these days and just shake my head. If they only realized the size of the diamond ring has nothing to do with the magnitude of the love and commitment they are receiving from their special someone.

Our romance definitely developed quickly. We met on February 1, 1980, were engaged by June and married in August. Rocke said if he could pick the date, I could pick the month. So he picked his favorite number, 22, and I chose August, my birthday month.   My parents were married on August 14, 1955; I was born on August 14, five years later. When I was very young, I envisioned my mom walking down the aisle in her white dress, very pregnant and then rushing off to the hospital to have me. It didn't' occur to me until I was a few years older that I had a big brother. My mom was married eight days after her 19th birthday; I was married eight days after my 20th birthday.   That was kind of a nice parallel. Mom and Dad celebrated their 25th wedding anniversary eight days before my wedding. We threw them a party that saw old friends from across the country travel to Pocatello for the special occasion.   So, between a wedding and a huge anniversary party, August of 1980 was a busy, busy month.

We had a lovely wedding in the church I attended as a child. It had a gorgeous, awe-inspiring sanctuary with wool burgundy carpet, dark oak pews and massive timber beams in the ceiling. The spectacular stained glass windows filtered the sunlight in rainbow rays throughout the chapel. We had an outside reception on the shady, front lawn of the church.

My best friend from college was my matron of honor. My cousin and my new sister-in-law were my bridesmaids. Rocke asked his youngest brother to be his best man and his other younger brother and my brother were his ushers.

Sweet little Jennifer was our flower girl. She was only three years old, and she forgot to throw the flower petals out of her basket on the way down the aisle. That just makes the memory that much more charming. I have never referred to Jennifer as my step daughter, she is just my daughter. We both had long blond hair and blue eyes. And in her teens, people sometimes thought we were sisters. That was always fun. If someone would comment that she looked like me, we would just smile, thank them and then giggle about it later.

Our wedding was small, simple and sweet-- perfect. We had a lot of music. My Aunt, who was an accomplished violinist, played the Lord's Prayer. We asked some of the Price family to be part of our special day too. Marilyn has a beautiful voice and sang "Sunrise, Sunset" from the film *Fiddler on the Roof*. My mom had always dreamed of having that special song in my wedding. We also asked Casey to play the guitar and sing Dan Fogelberg's popular song "Longer." It had become *our song* on our first ski date. We were listening to the radio as we were driving down the hill after a fun day of skiing and it was playing. Rocke said "I like this song." I said "Me too." That's all it took. We had a song.

I remember walking down the aisle, holding tight to my Dad's arm. I was smiling and not giving in to the urge to cry. I was so happy. As we passed by Chad, he had tears rolling down his cheeks. Seeing him so emotional caused both Dad and me to tear up a bit.

After the ceremony, we took off for our honeymoon in my dad's new Chevy pickup and camper. We drove 45 miles down the road to Lava Hot Springs, Idaho for our wedding night. We asked for the honeymoon suite, the clerk chuckled and said "We don't have a honeymoon suite but room number four has its own bathroom!" We took it. The staff was very thoughtful and kind and even delivered champagne to the room and made us feel special. That was the only night we spent in a hotel, we stayed in the camper the rest of the time and loved every second. We went up through Jackson Hole, Wyoming and West Yellowstone, Montana. We enjoyed the plays in Jackson Hole so much that we went back many times to celebrate anniversaries.

For our one-year anniversary, we loaded up the horses, Brandey and a mare named Lady that we had borrowed from Casey, and went camping up Scout Mountain, just south of Pocatello. We'd wrapped the top of our wedding cake in foil and stored it in the freezer. Tradition says, you're supposed to eat the top of your wedding cake on your first anniversary. So, we packed the foil wrapped cake in the cooler and took it with us. The first night, as we were getting dinner ready, I took the cake out. It was all soggy from being soaked in water from the melted ice in the bottom of the cooler. Oh well, the romantic intention was there.

We were married on August 22, 1980. Our wedding date is actually a palindrome; 082280, it is the same, whether read forward or backward. Pretty cool for a total coincidence!

The number 22 went on to be our family number. Years later when I received our two son's social security cards their numbers both had 22 in them. Our oldest son was number 22 for high school football. Several other incidents throughout our lives always came back to the number 22. The strangest one was the combination lock on the horse trailer spare tire. That first trailer, the one my parents had built for me in 1973. The combination was 0-22-0, how weird is that?

CHESSY-1981

Chapter 16

Rocke and TJ on Chessy, with Jennifer in 1984

We bought Chessy for Rocke soon after we were married. His only prerequisite was that his horse be a Palomino, seems he was fond of Trigger also. How interesting...

We started looking for the perfect Palomino and soon found Chessy Cha Cha, a three-year-old Quarter Horse mare. She was a dirty blond, meaning her yellow color had black hairs all through it. Her mane and tail were the signature bright white of palominos and she was built like a brick house. She was very stocky and well put together. She'd never been trained or handled much; in fact she hadn't ever been out of the field where we looked at her. Other than her feet being in desperate need of trimming, she was in pretty good shape and she seemed to have a nice disposition, so we bought her. We paid $1300.00 for her. Up to this point in my life she was, by far, the most expensive horse I had ever purchased. We loaded her (with a bit of difficulty) into the horse trailer and brought her home. We figured Rocke and I could train her and she'd be a great addition to our family. When I say home, I am referring to my parent's pasture. As newlyweds we were not yet in a financial position to be able to afford our own piece of land for the horses.

After we got her settled in with Brandey, we got busy with her training; she was fairly easy to train and was coming along nicely. One thing we hadn't counted on was that, even after we had her feet trimmed and shod, she walked with a paddle to her step because she was so used to walking around the platters that used to be her hooves. The other disappointing thing about her was her movement, she was very rough to ride, which was probably a side effect of her paddling gait.

Since we bought Chessy mainly so Rocke and I could go on romantic trail rides, we headed up the hills as soon as we felt she was ready. Chessy was doing great. She was sticking to the trail and walking along nice and relaxed. Better than Brandey--he was always a terrible trail horse. He was so nervous in the mountains that he jigged and jogged me until my innards were all tied in knots and my sides were aching. If the other horse, or group of horses, ever got out of his sight, he turned into a monster of constant angst, prancing and whinnying incessantly. Rocke had tied the saddlebags with our lunch to Chessy's saddle. After a while on the trail he dismounted to take a "rest." Something startled her. When she spooked, she jumped away from what scared her. That caused the saddlebags to bounce on her butt and flanks and that was all it took to send her flying! She took off bucking and kicking, with each stride causing her more grief from the bags. Rocke took out after her, but lost her quickly as she was running in panic. I stayed up on the trail looking for her. Brandey was doing his part by whinnying nonstop for over an hour. Rocke was about to give up the search when he sat down on a log in despair. When he looked up, there she was; worn out and wide eyed, waiting for him to rescue her from the monster that was tied to her saddle. Lesson learned; put the floppy saddlebags on the old, broke horse, not the colt that hadn't had the saddlebag lesson yet. She'd just been coming along so nicely, it was easy to forget that she was still young and inexperienced.

  One of our favorite lunch spots was a little hole in the wall called the Italian Place. They made awesome beef, mushroom and melted cheese sandwiches. We'd stopped there on our way up the mountain to buy sandwiches for lunch. By the time we captured our runaway lunch packer, our sandwiches were reduced to wads of thoroughly mixed ingredients all smashed into softball size globs. They were still tasty though...

At that point, I told Rocke the pudding story from my youth and we laughed as we enjoyed our lunch and each other. Seemed like a perfect Saturday to me!

CHACHI-1983

Chapter 17

Chachi in 1999 at 16 years old,
He still looked magnificent

Wow, where do I start with Chachi. I guess at the very beginning. Since Chessy wasn't really turning into the athletic horse we wanted (but she had excellent conformation with a big hind quarter), we decided to breed her to one of Price's excellent racing Quarter Horse studs. My hope was to get a speed horse with a powerful hind end to drive him around the barrels. Sir Aaron was the best, but so was the price tag on his breed fee. Hasten Jason was a stunning stud. He could've been the poster horse for The American Quarter Horse

Association. He was a deep, deep liver chestnut, with a brilliant blaze and white socks. Because he didn't have great success on the flat track, his breed fee was a little less. The problem with his races was this; he would break from the starting gate in the lead, but by the time he got to the last 100 yards, he would be approaching the grandstand and he hated the grandstand. He would start slowing down right before the finish line. Once, the jockey even tried a little buzzer to keep him going top speed through the finish line and past the grandstands. All that did was cause him to start bucking. He went on to have a pretty successful career as a chariot horse. Regardless of his lack of racing success, he was so gorgeous that I wanted to capture that beauty and speed in my own foal, so we opted to breed Chessy to him.

It was 1982, and I was pregnant with my first child. We actually bred Chessy late; in June. Most breeders of race horses like to breed earlier in the spring to give their colts an advantage of a few months when they begin racing as two year olds. No matter their actual birth date, all horses are considered born on January 1. The preferred breeding months were March, April and May. That way, the mare could deliver a foal anywhere from February to April. A mare's gestation period is eleven months, poor girls; I thought nine months was absolutely long enough! Since we didn't make the decision to breed Chessy until June, we were hoping that she would get pregnant the first try.

Chapter 18

Our first son, Thaddeas John Acree was born in late July. We called him TJ. (It turned out my pelvis injury was not a problem.)

TJ was born with "club feet." That basically meant the Achilles tendon on the back of his heels was too short and pulled his feet down and to the inside. While I was still in the hospital, an orthopedic surgeon came in to tell us that TJ would need correction on his feet immediately. After the shock of hearing our one-day old baby was not perfect and needed help, we soldiered on. The doctor placed tiny little casts on both feet. His bones were still so soft that the doctor could re-shape them with his hands. The doctor told us that he would change these casts every two weeks for about eight weeks.

Before TJ was born, we made the difficult decision to move back to Rocke's hometown of Nampa, Idaho, a suburb of Boise. We were struggling a bit financially, and Rocke had a good job opportunity in the Boise area.

TJ was born in July, and we moved in August. I borrowed one of Price's four-horse trailers and loaded up pretty much everything we owned. Rocke had already started his new job, so my mom and I drove the load to Nampa. We bought a fairly new 14 x 70 mobile home in a nice park. There was no acreage for the horses, so for the time being, we left Brandey and Chessy at my parent's place. That didn't last long. I couldn't be happy with my horses four hours away.

Rocke's parents had a small humble house on an acre lot. It had a run-in shed for shelter and was fenced. With my best puppy dog eyes, I asked my new in-laws if we could board the horses at their place. They said yes and we were off to retrieve the rest of our family. We still had the little 1973 horse trailer. Mom and Dad had given it to us when we got married. We loaded up Brandey and a hopefully pregnant Chessy and moved them to their new pasture in Nampa.

I had hoped I wouldn't have to go back to work for a while. I wanted to stay home with TJ for a few more months; he was only a month old when we moved. But, the reality of life was that I needed to go back to work. My best friend from college had moved to Boise to start her new job after we graduated. She actually moved while I was on my honeymoon! She had a line on a possible drafting job in Boise, so I dropped TJ off at his grandma's and drove to Boise for an interview.

After the interview, I went back to get TJ from Rocke's mom. As soon as I came in the door, I started crying. "Oh", she said "you didn't get the job." Through my tears, I sobbed "No, I did..."

Leaving TJ to go to work every morning was one of the hardest things I've ever had to do. At least he was with his grandmother. She had operated a daycare from her home for most of her life. Rocke tells stories of always having lots of kids to play with. That was in addition to his four brothers.

I settled in to working, but struggled with it. Since I was living in Nampa and working in Boise, 20 miles away, I would have to leave by 7:00 am. This meant for the most part, Rocke would take TJ to daycare. There were days that I didn't get to see my baby until almost 6:00 pm.

Since I wasn't able to breastfeed anymore, we started TJ on formula, not knowing that he wasn't going to be able to adjust to the change. My poor boy, he was allergic to every kind of formula we tried. One evening we were sitting in Rocke's parent's living room just visiting with his family. I was holding TJ on my knees facing out toward everyone. All of sudden, I felt his tummy roll and in an instant he was throwing up the latest brand of formula we'd tried. Projectile like...clear across the room. Rocke's brothers started laughing because it was quite a sight. Rocke's dad, Bud, stood up and roared at us all, "You shouldn't be laughing at that poor baby, he's sick." Bud stormed upstairs and we all felt properly chastened.

That started a long and extremely frustrating search for something that TJ could eat and keep down. I kept taking him to the pediatrician only to be told to give him Pedialite. At that time, Pedialite was essentially just water with added minerals. It had nothing in it that could sustain a baby. TJ was losing weight and strength at an alarming rate. His eyes looked sunken and his complexion was pasty. During one of our first visits to the doctor, he had mentioned a meat based formula we might try if nothing else worked. Well, nothing else was working! I insisted, not so politely, that he prescribe the meat-based formula.

Immediately after starting the new formula, TJ started to improve. The color came back to his cheeks. His eyes brightened up. And, he started growing and gaining his weight back. The only negative to this formula was that it came out of the can smelling like cat food, with a sickening slimy texture. I could be seen gagging at the sink if I accidently dripped some on my hands while making up a bottle. It was worth it; my energetic boy was back! After a month or so, TJ was crawling around with the bottle in his teeth, growling....after all, it was meat based!

Before we left Pocatello, TJ's casts had been changed twice. He still needed two more changes. Since we'd moved to Nampa, I had to go back to Pocatello for his doctor's appointments. We only had one reliable car and Rocke needed it for work, so I took the train. Nampa and Pocatello are railroad towns, so Amtrak ran through both of them.

I remember having to board the Nampa train at 2:00 am. There wasn't even a depot, we just walked out to the tracks and got on the train. TJ was now six weeks old. Since it was the middle of the night, we both slept most of the way. I didn't have any problems with him on the train and the trip went smoothly. My parents picked us up at the railroad station about 6:30 that morning, and it was a joyful reunion. We had only been gone for a couple of weeks, but we were still struggling with the separation. It seemed every time we visited, when it was time to leave, our goodbyes were always tearful. I had never been more than a few minutes away from my folks and this new phase of my life was going to take some getting used to, by all of us.

I took TJ to the appointment. We joked that since he'd had casts on since he was a day old, his feet would probably just rise up in the air after the heavy casts were removed. Well, they did! It was a pretty funny sight, this tiny baby, with his legs defying gravity and just floating up. The doctor decided since we'd moved and it was difficult to get back for these cast changes that we could probably forego the last set of casts. He sent us home with the hope that the reshaping of his feet would remain firm and that would be all the treatment he would need. That was a naïve hope, as it turned out.

TJ would go on to have corrective shoes and short leg braces for almost his entire first year. On a positive note, his legs were so strong from all of the hardware, he walked at eight months.

I was always grateful that it was the latter part of the 20th century. If he had been born in earlier times, he would have been crippled. Thank goodness for modern medical progress!

By the time he was four, it was evident that we needed to find a physical activity or sport for him to participate in. Wrestling was the only thing available, so we started him there. He was the youngest competitor by two years, but he needed an outlet for his endless and infinite energy. At one memorable practice, TJ started crying when another boy held him down on the mat. On their way home, Rocke scolded TJ and told him "You tell Mom that you have to have a nap on wrestling days, no more crying!" The next weekend at the competition, the boy he was wrestling started to cry as TJ held him pinned to the mat. Without letting his opponent up, he hollered "Hey Dad, I guess he didn't have a nap!" Everyone got a chuckle out of that, except the poor boy he had pinned. Thankfully, that was the only year we had to endure those extremely long Saturdays in stale smelling gyms watching a sport that I disliked immensely. The aroma of fifty sweaty little boys is fairly putrid. The next spring, he was eligible to play on a U-6 (under six years old) soccer team and our spectator venue was moved to the crisp green soccer fields in the great outdoors. We took incredible pleasure in the fresh, clean air that we could willingly deeply inhale.

TJ grew up to be a phenomenal athlete. He played whatever sport was in season and was exceptionally good at all of them, just like his dad. He went on to play football for the mighty Boise State Broncos. After one especially outstanding game, my niece was flipping through her dad's ESPN magazine. She started squealing in excitement "TJ is in ESPN! TJ's picture is in this magazine!" I must admit it was awfully fun having a celebrity in the family. His junior year, he was named Player of the Game by ESPN for his outstanding performance in the Fort Worth Bowl. He was the Western Athletic Conference (WAC) *Player of the Week* twice and named as wide receiver to the All-

Conference Team his senior year. TJ was then signed by the Canadian Football League team, the BC Lions. He played for British Columbia for two years and then went to the Edmonton Eskimos. He had an amazing start to his first season with the Eskimos. He was actually the CFL's leading receiver after the second game of the season.

Unfortunately, his feet had always been a bit fragile and after so many years of taking a beating by playing football at such high levels, he was forced to retire after his fifth season in the CFL. His feet kept developing stress fractures. He just could not keep them healthy and uninjured.

He had an amazing football career and we loved every minute of it. We traveled to most of the BSU games and even made it up to Canada three times. We visited Vancouver, British Columbia, Edmonton, Alberta and Toronto, Ontario during his CFL career. Not bad, eh? Just a little Canadian humor...very little, I know.

Chapter 19

Chessy was due to deliver her foal in late April or early May. Since I was working in Boise, I was a fretful, anxious wreck waiting for her to go into labor. I so wanted to be there for the birth, but of course, the chances of that were slim.

I got the call at work. Rocke announced we had a cute little sorrel filly with a blaze and white socks on her legs. Although I was happy and relieved to have a healthy baby, I was disappointed for a couple of other reasons. First, I missed it. I had never witnessed a foal's birth firsthand and felt it was a significant article missing from my life's story line so far. Second, the baby was a filly (a female foal). I really had my heart set on a horse colt (a male foal) as I had the perfect name picked out. Rocke's brother, Jeff had luckily been close at hand to help Chessy deliver. His mom was there too, offering whatever advice she could from her experience as a mother. Evidently, Jeff was much better at finance than zoology.

I hurried home from work to see our new addition. Rocke had arrived before me and was out with the horses. I gave the foal a quick once over then with a happy smile and a knowing chuckle asked Rocke, "Did you look at this foal? She's a boy!"

We had a bouncing baby colt on May 5, 1983. He was our Cinco de Mayo foal.

Chad worked for Union Pacific Railroad and his usual route at that time was from Pocatello to Nampa and back. He dropped by to see us and inspect our future superstar. Chachi was just a few days old when Chad came to check him out. He seemed pleased with what he saw and told us "Looks like you got a good one!"

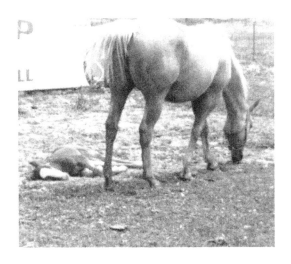

Chessy and baby Chachi-1983

His official registered name with the American Quarter Horse Association was 'Like a Rocket's Chachi.' Hasten Jason's sire was Like a Rocket. I loved Scott Bao's character from the TV show *Happy Days* and since his dam's name was Chessy Cha Cha, *Chachi* was *the* perfect name for him.

We only stayed in Nampa for about a year. We just weren't happy there. My mom mentioned that Marilyn had told her that the semiconductor plant, AMI, where she worked in Pocatello, was hiring. I had her send applications for both of us. I thought I might be hired as a drafter; I had a pretty good amount of experience. We weren't sure what kind of positions the company was looking to fill. I completed the applications, attached our resumes and sent them in. Rocke had a few years' experience working for the water department for the City of Pocatello.

AMI, American Microsystems, hired Rocke to build the chemical distribution system for the entire plant. We had written Marilyn down as a reference and when they called to ask her about Rocke, she told them, "He was a talented and skilled young man and they better not let him get away!" After all these years, the Price family was still looking out for me and helping to form my life.

Rocke ended up 'climbing the corporate ladder' and working for AMI for over 20 years. Rather than going back to drafting when we returned to Pocatello, I decided to try my hand at Real Estate so I would have a more flexible schedule. So, I signed up for the class, took the test, passed it, and became a Realtor.

After we moved back to Pocatello from Nampa, we had to keep Brandey, Chessy and baby Chachi at my parent's place once again.

We were finally able to get a place of our own with acreage for the horses in 1984. It was located on Buckskin Road in the mountains east of Pocatello. It was an old, 1972 double-wide mobile home nestled up in the trees sitting on three acres, most of it mountainside. We didn't care. It was gorgeous up there and we were ready to build fence and have the horses live with us.

While living on Buckskin, I met a young woman that would become my best friend for the next 30 years (and counting). Char and I actually met while we both were working at an upscale restaurant; she, as a server and I, as the weekend bookkeeper. While sitting at the bar visiting with her after work one evening, I learned that she had a horse and lived on Buckskin Road. I suggested we get together and go for a ride together sometime. She replied that she didn't have a horse trailer and I told her that wouldn't be a problem because we had recently moved in to Old Mr. Moon's place on Buckskin just below the ski area. That's all it took, our friendship was born.

Char and her husband, Larry, lived just down the road from us. She had a little black and white mare that she called Kahlua. Over the six years we lived there, we enjoyed many a ride through the mountain trails near our homes.

We witnessed many amazing sunsets from up on the mountain. Vibrant reds and oranges filled the sky at dusk. We could often be found sitting on the deck basking in the breathtaking view on summer evenings. In the fall, the turning leaves on the thick trees looked like orange and yellow cotton candy, lining the gullies and topping the ridges.

Char and Larry did not have children, and every so often, they would borrow ours for the night. They would pick them up in their trademark four-wheel drive, olive green Subaru station wagon. Then, they would grab a pizza and head out to one of the local Drive-In Theaters. Remember, it was the 1980s. They always treated our boys and Jennifer like they were the best and brightest kids they knew. I always appreciated Char and Larry for the kindness and regard they offered all of our children. Our family was very fortunate that just by chance, a simple part-time job connected us with these energetic, generous and considerate friends.

Chapter 20

Because our acreage was steep, and we had no way to irrigate it, we still occasionally kept the horses at Mom and Dad's.

My mom was in the habit of mowing the yard on Wednesdays and tossing the lawn clippings over the fence for the horses to munch on. I happened to be at their place one Wednesday and a yard maintenance man came to the door and said he'd just sprayed their lawn by mistake. He was supposed to have sprayed the yard next door. I told him, that it was probably not a problem unless he'd sprayed my mom's prize garden. He said, that no, he'd just done the lawn. I called Dad and let him know what'd happened.

Mom came home from work and mowed the lawn as usual. Not aware of the accidental spraying, she dumped the clippings over the corral fence. Chessy was kind of a piggy eater and she ate a lot of the pile. Brandey didn't care for grass clippings and Chachi's baby teeth weren't developed enough for him to eat much.

The next morning, Mom called in a panic and told me Chessy looked awful. She said she was a muddy mess and kept lying down and getting up. I called the Veterinarian whose clinic was just across the street from my parent's house and she said she would meet me there.

When I arrived, it was an awful sight. Chessy was covered with filthy sweat. Her head was caked with dirt and even her ears were full of mud. It looked like she had been violently rolling all night. The Vet called the lawn company to find out what chemicals were in the spray that had been used. After she got that information, she called the poison hotline for the best way to treat this kind of poisoning in a horse.

She administered charcoal through a nose tube directly into her stomach to try to absorb the toxic chemicals. She also gave her an injection of something to make her more comfortable and ease the pain. Rocke came out, and we all worked diligently, trying to save our sweet mare. After several hours, it became inevitable that Chessy was going to die. I was so upset I retreated like a coward into the house. When it came to sadness and the suffering of my animals, I just had no inner strength to get through these difficult and heart wrenching times. So, again, I left Rocke to deal with the awful and dreaded reality of losing a beloved pet.

Later that night, the yard worker that had sprayed the yard and his boss showed up at the door to apologize and to tell us they would pay the Vet bill. We told them that Chessy had died just a little bit earlier. The worker was in tears. He was so sorry for the mistake. In the end, he got fired, which I didn't believe was necessary. He probably would have been their most reliable and conscientious worker after that experience. They paid us $1200.00 for Chessy, plus the Vet and disposal bills. This was our first experience with having one of our horses die and no amount of money would ease the pain.

We had to have some men with a dump truck and backhoe come to the pasture to take Chessy away. There really wasn't much choice of where to dispose of a horse carcass in Pocatello, so they took her to the landfill that had a section specifically designated for dead animals. I stopped out between work appointments to see if they'd taken Chessy away yet. Unfortunately, I got there just as they were loading her body into the truck. Not a pretty sight. I wish I'd stayed away so I didn't have that vision stuck in my head.

The price we pay for loving these wonderful animals is having to deal with losing them. Grief is grief, no matter for whom or what we are grieving.

Chessy at our home in the mountains, 1984

Chapter 21

Chachi was a great little colt. When I say little, I mean that literally. He'd inherited his sire's beautiful color, but not his size. His sorrel fuzzy baby coat was replaced by a deep chestnut. He also inherited his mother's substantial hind quarter, but he only grew to be about 14.1 hands tall. With a hand being four inches, he stood less than 60 inches at his wither. He was small, but he was mighty...exceptionally fast and athletic!

I wanted Chachi to be my next barrel and pole bending horse. By the time Chachi was three, I'd passed Brandey down to my children. Brandey was now 13. Jennifer started 4-H with him in 1986, when she was nine years old.

Jennifer and Brandey at the County 4-H Fair in 1986

Jennifer enjoyed great success with Brandey in 4-H for five years. By her fourth year in 4-H, she was 12 years old and had developed into a beautiful rider. She and Brandey were a great team. By the end of the

County Fair that year, she had won four classes; Western and Bareback Equitation, Pole Bending and Barrel Racing. We still have the blankets that were awarded to the first place contestant in each class. It seemed they could do no wrong in the eyes of the judge that year. Jennifer was focused in her cues and Brandey responded flawlessly. Of course, it was a very fun year for this proud mom.

Our second son, Zack was born that summer in June. We were still living on Buckskin Road and sometimes Char and I would haul the horses down to ride in the arenas at the fairgrounds. As soon as he could sit up and before he could even walk, I would take Zack on horseback rides, he would sit in the saddle in front of me. He loved it and I loved having him with me. He was clearly going to be my little cowboy.

TJ and Zack also got to compete with Brandey. TJ was only about seven years old when he ran poles on Brandey. TJ hit the end pole with his head because Brandey had wrapped around it so tight. When he finished his run and trotted out of the arena, he had a big knot on his forehead. Now that is a tight turning pole horse!

When Zack was four, he competed in a little horse show with his five-year-old friend Lisa. Lisa was riding her older sister's horse too. Her name was Lady. It was just a walk/trot class, and Zack and Lisa somehow got their stirrups stuck together. Brandey and Lady just trotted around the arena, taking care of their two tiny passengers.   It was as if they were telling each other, "Keep it smooth and calm so our precious cargo stays safe and secure."   Children and horses make for some wonderful, cherished memories.

Brandey and Zack in 1990
Brandey was 17 and Zack was just 4 years old

Since Brandey had a new gig as a kid's horse, I gave my full attention to getting Chachi finished as a barrel horse.   My goal was to get Chachi to the "open" level of competition.   Until a horse had won at least $500, he was considered a "novice horse."   I continued competing and winning some pretty good payouts.   The next year, we finally reached our goal.

Chapter 22

Because of the amount of money Chachi had won, he was now classified as an "open" or in other words, a professional barrel horse. I had always wanted to barrel race in Rodeos. After attaining valuable experience running at jackpots, I started competing at some small town rodeos in 1991. We were having fun and making a little money too.

I was competing in a rodeo in Swan Valley, Idaho. Because we were expecting out-of-town guests for the weekend, Mom and Dad drove over with me while Rocke and the kids stayed home to get ready for our visitors.

It was a beautiful day; the sun was shining, although it wasn't too hot. Swan Valley has an awe-inspiring view of the Teton Mountains. Every time I drive down into that glorious valley, the view takes my breath away. I always look forward to coming over the steep mountain pass and gazing down onto the bright green, lush pastures dotted with cattle and horses.

As we were warming up our horses before the rodeo, some of the other barrel racers and I were commenting on how we would hate to be a bull or bronc rider that day. The arena seemed unusually hard and was not worked well. We laughed and talked about how we wouldn't want to land on that hard packed ground. Our conversation turned out to be prophetic.

As I watched the barrel racers before me, the times seemed pretty fast, so I was looking forward to having an excellent run.

I ran into the arena and set up for the first barrel. Everything felt great. My pocket was tight and my turn fast. On to the second barrel and again, I felt I was having a great run. As I started into the pocket of the third and final barrel, something was wrong. I was still in the saddle but Chachi was getting farther and farther away from me. Since I had a hold of his head via the reins, I was pulling him over on top of me.

When I finally realized what was happening, I released him immediately, and I came off. The offside billet of my saddle, the piece of leather holding the cinch to the saddle, had broken. Yes, I was staying in the saddle but the saddle wasn't staying on Chachi's back. I hit hard, landing on my right hip. I struggled to look over my shoulder to see if Chachi was alright. He was trotting to the fence with the saddle hanging on the side of him, held only by the breast collar.

I tried sitting up, but couldn't feel my legs. I lay back down and the paramedics rushed to me in the arena. Again, I tried to move, but just felt numb. They brought in a backboard and neck brace. When they tried to put the neck brace on I said, "I can guarantee it's not my neck, it's my ass!" I know, not a very nice thing to say. But, I wasn't feeling very nice at the time.

They got me on the backboard and into the ambulance. It took well over an hour to get to the Idaho Falls hospital. Fortunately, the numbness started to go away and I could feel below my waist again. Having feeling was good, but the feeling was pain, not so good.

Even through the throbbing and jabbing pains, I worried about Chachi and my parents all the way to the hospital.

An official in the arena caught Chachi and took him to the gate. He was all right, just a little shaken up with all the commotion. My mom went to the gate to retrieve him and a nice old cowboy helped get him unsaddled, unbridled and loaded into the trailer.

Dad parked the horse trailer, with Chachi inside, in the parking lot at the hospital. By the time they made it to the hospital and found me, I had already been to x-ray. The doctor said I had a hairline fracture of my hip. He wasn't too worried about that; there really wasn't much he could do. I just needed to give it time to heal. What he was really concerned about was that my pelvis was extremely shifted. I laughed...which hurt. Through a wince I said "Oh, that didn't happen today, that's an old injury!" Remember Brandey and the scary saddle pad? The doctor was amazed that I'd been living with it so off-kilter for so long. He sent me home with crutches. Again with the crutches! He gave me pain medication, something with codeine in it and told me to go straight to bed when I got home. My pain, or lack of, would be the deciding factor on how soon I could ride again.

We got home late that night. Dad drove. They dropped me off at home, and then took the truck, trailer and Chachi back to their place. Rocke, the kids and his brother and sister-in-law were at our house anxiously waiting for us. This was before the days of cell phones, so they'd just received the one call from Mom when we were at the hospital.

I settled into bed, I was exhausted and hurting. It was then that I realized I must be allergic to codeine because I was sick and nauseous. What a miserable night, I was obviously not a very good hostess to our guests.

I was out of commission for over a month. I crutched around until I couldn't stand it for another minute. So, I "Cowgirled Up!" as they say, and got back in the saddle. A recently repaired saddle, that is.

Injuries to competitors in all rodeo events are common. Most people don't think about Pole Bending and Barrel Racing as sports with the potential for injury. But speaking from experience, nothing hurts quite like hitting a rock-hard pole with your kneecap at 35 miles per hour, unless maybe it's slicing your shin open on the edge of a metal barrel with the force of a 1000-pound animal behind it. My legs still bear the numerous scars of my competition days. It seems strange to say, but those bruises and lacerations and the unique kind of pain that accompanied them, made me feel alive and declared that I was living life to the fullest!

Chapter 23

In 1989, we decided it was time to move off the mountain and become flatlanders. TJ was getting to an age where he was in so many activities that making several trips a day, up and down the long and winding road to our place was becoming too much. We also wanted an irrigated pasture for the horses. I thought it would be great to have an arena of my own in which to train and host jackpots.

We made an offer on a house with three acres after we sold our place on Buckskin. Our offer was accepted and we were given permission to start moving our things into the garage of the new house. The house already had an offer on it, but it was contingent on the other buyers selling their home first. All of the realtors involved assured us that there was no way the other buyers could remove the contingency in the allowed three days. At the last possible moment, just minutes before midnight on the third night, we got a call from our realtor telling us that the other buyers had come up with some very *creative* financing and were removing their contingency. We were homeless. We were so disappointed. We removed our belongings that we had already taken to the new house and stored them in my parent's garage, then, while living in their basement, hurriedly looked for a place to live. We ended up buying a house in a nearby neighborhood, because we just weren't able to quickly find another home on acreage that we liked and could afford. While living in the house in town, we continued to look for our perfect forever home.

We finally decided we wanted to build our new place from start to finish, that way it would be exactly what we wanted. We purchased five acres of lush, irrigated pastureland on Whitaker Road, just north of Pocatello, in 1991. That first year, we built the fence. White vinyl fence was just being introduced. We ordered 1000 feet of three rail fencing from a company in Syracuse, NY. That amount of fencing was enough for an arena and a couple of corrals and a small pasture. We fenced the rest of the land with wooden posts and smooth twisted wire, no barbs! I absolutely hate barbed wire. If you've ever witnessed what those ripping barbs do to horse hide, you would agree. No horse should ever be fenced in with barbed wire! Okay, I'll step down off of my soapbox now.

We would have liked to surround all five acres with the nice white vinyl fencing, but that just wasn't in the budget.

That first year, even though we didn't yet live on our property, we still pastured the horses there during the summer. The new acreage was about three miles from my parent's place, where we had been boarding the horses, off and on, over the years.

The first time we left Brandey and Chachi at the new pasture alone, they somehow escaped. I went out to check on them after work and they were nowhere to be found. I tried not to panic and quickly hooked up my little horse trailer. I figured they might head towards my folk's place so, I started that direction. Unfortunately, that route crossed railroad tracks and a busy highway.

As I drove, my stomach felt sick with worry. I searched the surrounding fields. I crossed the RR tracks and the highway and still no sign of my run-away horses. I was actually relieved not to see them running down the highway. I continued on, with the hope that they were going back to their familiar pasture. I struggled to keep the rising panic I was feeling at bay.

About a quarter of a mile before the turn onto the road that my parent's house was on, there they were. They were trotting down the middle of the road. I pulled up behind them and stopped the truck. As I jumped out, I yelled their names. They stopped and turned around to me. I said "Brandey, load up!" I didn't even put his halter on him. I just opened the trailer gate and he jumped in. I told Chachi the same thing, after closing Brandey's side. He too, jumped right in. No halter or lead rope on either of them. They were both dripping with sweat and so relieved to be safe in their trailer.

By this time, cars had stopped on the road in front of and behind us. Nobody got out of their cars to help me. I think they were all dumbstruck. They just sat and watched in disbelief, as my escapees loaded themselves into the trailer.

Having a genuine partnership with your horses, and have them look to you for safety and leadership is priceless. The close bond I shared with my horses was very apparent on the road that evening.

I hauled them home and they were clearly happy to be back in the safety and security of a fenced pasture. After that escapade, we secured the gates with double latches and checked them twice. We definitely did not want a repeat adventure.

In January of 1992, we started construction on our dream home. I designed it with input from Rocke and the kids and a two-man startup construction company built it for us. We did anything and everything we could, to help lower costs. Rocke did all of the plumbing and electrical. Also, with the help of my ever supportive mom and dad, we painted every wall and stained all of the doors, baseboards and trim. It wasn't big or fancy, but it was ours and we loved it.

Over the summer of 1992, we added the barn. Since we didn't know how to set up concrete foundation forms, we built the foundation using cinder blocks. It was at this time that I realized Rocke was a bit of a perfectionist. When we set a level on the foundation wall, there was less than 1/8 of an inch difference in the height of all four corners; pretty good for amateurs. Our new barn had three spacious stalls, a tack room and a doctoring chute/hitching post that Chad had built for me. It also stored about 10 tons of hay.

We finally had a place of our own; one where we could raise our children and give them a country lifestyle. A home where they could learn how to work hard and have the space to play even harder. And, we could finally have all of our critters live with us full time.

The custom home we built on Whitaker Rd
Five acres of lush pasture, barn, corrals and an arena.
What more could a girl want?

Chapter 24

I continued to run at jackpots, small town rodeos and other barrel competitions. Then in 1992, I decided Chachi and I were having enough success to start competing at the next level. I joined the Intermountain Professional Rodeo Association. They held rodeos all over Idaho, western Wyoming, and northern Utah and Nevada.

Chachi and I started our first professional rodeo season off well. We'd been in the top ten at all of the rodeos we entered. Although, we still hadn't earned a check. It seemed if they paid six places, we were seventh, if they paid three, we were fourth, so frustrating. We needed to make some money because each rodeo had an entry fee of anywhere from $50 to $100. That was just for the privilege of running. We finally had our biggest success at the Fourth of July Rodeo in Rupert, Idaho. Rocke's mom and brothers and their families were all visiting that weekend from Nampa, so they all came over to watch me compete at the rodeo. It was a little unnerving to have such an intimate audience, but also exciting.

Competition always caused me to have butterflies in my stomach. I felt confident that we could compete at this level, but I still had pre-run jitters. Sometimes, when I was driving to a rodeo, I would listen to Garth Brooks' Rodeo song and belt out the chorus at the top of my lungs. "Well it's bulls and blood, it's dust and mud, it's the roar of the Sunday crowd, it's the white in his knuckles, the gold in the buckle, he'll win the next go round, it's boots and chaps, it's cowboy hats, it's spurs and latigo, it's the ropes and the reins, and the joy and the pain, and they call the thing Rodeoowowo!" My somewhat off-key and loud rendition seemed to help expel some of my nervous energy.

On this night, my stomach butterflies seemed particularly active and fluttery.

I remember running in to the arena, setting up and turning the first barrel and having it feel absolutely perfect. So far so good, just as we were coming out of the turn at the second barrel heading for the third, I distinctly remember hearing the announcer say something about my "big, stout chestnut horse" ...what barrel race was he watching? Chachi was anything but big and stout. All I can think, is he saw his impressive hind quarters powering away from the barrel and figured that rear end could only belong to a big horse. Our time was 17.51 seconds on a full set. That was our fastest time ever on a full set of barrels. We were sitting in first place and I nervously watched each girl run, and then listened for her time to be announced. Every time, letting out my held breath and a sigh of relief as each time was slower than mine.

When the barrels were over, I was still in the lead and Jennifer came running out of the stands, smiling and shouting "You Won! You Won!"

Even though I had won that performance, the go round included slack runs. During a rodeo performance, the time allowed for each event limits how many competitors can actually run in the show. Any extra racers have to run in what is called slack. Sometimes slack is run in the morning before the rodeo, other times it is run after the rodeo. This time it was late that night, after the rodeo. I had to wait until the next day to find out what the times had been in slack. A friend that was in the break-away calf roping slack called me the next day to tell me I ended up second. The last girl to run had beaten my time by less than a tenth of a second. Barrel races are decided by hundredths of a second. It is a sport decided by the tiniest of margins. A slip at a barrel can be the difference between a paycheck and a long, unhappy ride home.

My first check was about $800.00. Whew! I could afford to enter another rodeo.

Since it was my first season as a professional, I was considered a Rookie. There was a Rookie of the Year Buckle given at the year-end awards banquet. I was a fairly old rookie at 32. All season I'd been trading places in the rookie standings with a girl fresh out of high school.

We both made it to the IMPRA Finals; whoever did better at the Finals, would win the rookie buckle. Nerves got the better of me and I didn't let Chachi do his thing. I'd been watching the competitors before me and they were all taking a really big pocket at the first barrel. A pocket is the amount of space away from the barrel on the backside before you turn it. As I ran to the first barrel

I adjusted Chachi over away from the barrel...he didn't need that big pocket...what was I thinking? I wasn't. That move disrupted his momentum and cost us time. We had a disappointing time and lost out on the rookie award. Rocke felt so bad for me that he gave me a nice new buckle. I told him it wasn't about the buckle. I loved the fact that he cared so much that he bought me one anyway. He was always so supportive of me in everything I did. He was my Rock. His confidence in me helped build the self-confidence I'd been lacking most of my life.

In barrel racing and pole bending, the fastest time will win. It is not judged under any subjective points of view, only the clock. I always loved this about these sports. No judge's opinion can ruin your day. I had to rely on my horse and he had to trust me unconditionally. The bonds that are formed with these amazing equine athletes must be strong. You are depending on them to rev up to a high adrenaline frame of mind, to carry you on an extremely fast course and then return to a calm state and quietly walk out of the arena. Oftentimes, after my run, Chachi could be seen with one of the kid's riding him to cool him down. He was truly a reliable horse.

Susan and Chachi at a Barrel Race
August, 1994 near Reno Nevada

Rocke and the kids would usually go with me to my rodeos, but once in a while, schedules would conflict and I would either go alone or only one of them would join me. On one particular weekend, TJ was the elected companion. The rodeo was about two hours north of Pocatello. I remember pulling in to the rodeo grounds and TJ got out and helped me get Chachi ready to run, then, rather than come in to watch the rodeo, he just crawled in the backseat of our Ford Bronco and went to sleep. After my run, I returned to the trailer, unsaddled Chachi, cooled him down and loaded up to go home. When I climbed in the Bronco, TJ woke up and asked "Did you win?" I appreciated him going with me so I didn't have to drive all the way alone, but he was not much of a rodeo fan.

I hadn't won. It was an indoor arena and the ground was so deep, Chachi could not dig his way out of the ground at each barrel. I told TJ it felt like he was running on toothpicks. Chachi was so small I usually did well on the short sets that are common in indoor arenas. But because his feet and hoof contact area matched his size, he also did better when he could run more on top of the ground. Arenas that had been worked and dug really deep were a big disadvantage for my little horse.

I only competed in rodeos with the IMPRA that one year. Jennifer and the boys were getting older and there just didn't seem to be enough time for everyone's activities. And, as all parents know, our children come first. I continued to run at jackpots closer to home when I could fit them in, but the time of our watching TJ in every sport available to him was starting in full force. Zack and Jennifer competed on Brandey at some jackpots and that was always good family fun too.

Chapter 25

Foxy and newborn Sly

In 1989, Rocke's best friend, Bill had been given two Appaloosa horses as payment for some work he had done.

He asked if I'd take them, see what kind of training they had (if any) and determine if they were good riding horses. The gelding was a good sized horse and seemed like he might make a good hunting horse. The mare, Foxy, unfortunately had an old injury that caused her to be quite lame in one knee.

Bill had jokingly named them Alpo and Purina. I didn't find this at all funny.

Foxy was a very pretty horse and had excellent conformation. She was chestnut in color and had a bright white blanket over her hindquarters. This is the marking that most appaloosas are recognized for.

Since she couldn't be ridden, Bill was talking about shipping her off to a rendering plant. A rendering plant is nothing more than a slaughterhouse that uses horsemeat and the rest of the carcass for things such as glue and dog food.

I couldn't stand the thought of that, so I asked if I could keep her and breed her to get a nice Appaloosa/Quarter Horse foal. I told him that if we got a good colt, he could probably sell Foxy as a broodmare. He agreed. Bill has been one of the people in our lives that we have truly treasured. He is generous with his time, friendship and heartfelt laughter.

Chad still had Sir Aaron standing at stud at the ranch, so we decided to breed Foxy to him. Chad had a two-year-old colt that needed to be started under saddle. So, we traded a breed fee to Sir Aaron for 30 days training from me on his colt.

Foxy was easy to breed and "caught" right away. When a mare is in heat it means her cycle is such that she is open to getting pregnant. During a mare's heat, she will usually be bred every other day for eight to twelve days. To say that she caught right away just means that she became pregnant in the first heat cycle that we bred her.

We anxiously awaited the arrival of the new foal. I was hoping for a colt again. I've always preferred geldings (neutered males) over mares. Geldings are less moody than mares and are easier to get along with on a more consistent basis, and, of course, for me, easier to fall in love with.

Since Aaron was black, I had visions of a beautiful black colt with a flashy white blanket over his rump. I got the call that Foxy was in labor and having a little bit of difficulty progressing with the birth. I immediately called the Veterinarian and she met me at the pasture. There was excitement in the air, but also some trepidation. Foal birth, as with childbirth is a complicated ordeal. My emotions leading up to this birth had been all over the place. I was excited and thrilled that we were going to have another baby. I was also full of fear and anxiety that something might go wrong and we might lose both mare and foal. I vowed that this would be the last time we bred one of our mares to get another foal. I figured there were enough horses in the world already. If we wanted another foal, we could buy one. Then, I'd be sure to get a colt to my liking without all the worry.

The Vet and I arrived to find Foxy down with a tiny hoof sticking out of the birth canal. My mom said she'd been that way for at least 20 minutes so the Vet decided Foxy needed some assistance delivering the foal.

As the doctor got her equipment ready, Foxy stood up. This kind of freaked me out, why on earth would she want to have a baby standing up? The Vet said this was normal when a mare was uncomfortable and unable to complete the birth.

This actually made it easier for her to get a rope looped over both tiny feet and secured. As she stepped back and started pulling on the rope, she told me to grab the legs, as best I could, to help pull. Just as we started to pull in earnest, Foxy had a big contraction and strong push. All while she was still standing!

Foxy pushed, we pulled and out slid an adorable, but wet, black foal. I had just turned to ask if I should try to catch the foal when ..."Ker plunk" ...it landed on the ground.

After the initial shock of having a foal land on my feet, I was thrilled. The tiny foal *was* black with a fantastic white blanket on the butt! The Vet cleaned out the baby's nose and mouth and it started being pretty active right away. I couldn't wait to turn the new foal over and see what gender it was. Could we be so lucky as to have another stud colt? Yes! Hallelujah, we got another boy! He seemed perfect, in addition to his black color and blanket; he had a tiny white star on his forehead, just like his sire, Sir Aaron. We named him Sly Like a Fox, Sly for short.

Luckily, unlike when Chachi was born, I was able to be present and witness this miracle. I can check this wonderful, exciting entry off my bucket list. It was so fun to watch those first wobbly steps. He tried to gain his feet a few times without success. He would sway one way and then the other and fall over each time. He'd rest for a few minutes in between attempts and then Foxy would encourage him, as only a mamma can, to try again, gently nudging him with her nose.

The first milk from the mare is called colostrum. Colostrum is very high in proteins and other nutrients which provide the foal with resistance to infections and diseases. It is important that the newborn foal starts to nurse soon after birth to get the most benefit from the colostrum.

Foxy was having a hard time getting Sly to nurse. She would use her soft muzzle to guide him back to her udder, but he wasn't able to latch on to a teat and nurse. We decided to bottle feed him for the first few hours with a milk substitute.

On his way over with Jennifer and the boys, Rocke stopped at the feed store to get a foal bottle and nipple and the supplement. This was going to be Jennifer's first experience doctoring a newborn foal. She was a natural.

Jennifer and Rocke bottle feeding Baby Sly

When Jennifer was just nine years old, she made the proclamation that she was going to be a Veterinarian. I'd also had that aspiration when I was young, but life and its obstacles have a way of changing our dreams. So, I told her, "That's great! Straight 'A's, No boys."

She was determined to accomplish her lifelong dream and she made it look easy. I'd like to think it was my wise words that helped pave the way, but I'm pretty sure it was just her amazing "Do what it takes" attitude that drove her to attain such a lofty goal.

Jennifer graduated from Oregon State University as a Doctor of Veterinary Medicine with academic honors in 2003.

She wanted to be a "horses only" Vet. No cows or cats! Although, I do remember getting a phone call from her during Vet school wanting us to adopt a sheep that had been used by the program. Rocke said "Sure, I didn't know you liked lamb chops!" Not surprisingly, the sheep did not come to live with us. Jennifer had been a vegetarian since she was barely a teenager.

After graduation, the first equine-only offer she received was from a clinic in Pennsylvania. She'd spent her entire life in Idaho and Oregon. She was hesitant to move across the country to such an unknown area. We encouraged her to give it try, maybe she would love the east coast. She didn't.

Jennifer joined a Veterinary practice that served a very rural area outside of Philadelphia. The weather was brutal; humid and freezing at the same time in the winter and suffocatingly hot in the summer. The area was also so rural, that it took her over an hour to drive to a restaurant or grocery store. She was a country girl, but that was ridiculous.

During that first year in Pennsylvania, Jennifer kept up her search for an Equine Practice closer to home. A position opened up back in Oregon. She flew back for an interview and the clinic's Veterinarian/owner hired her on the spot. Jennifer got married in 2004, so she and her new husband, Ben, made the cross country trip, one more time in February of 2005.

Chapter 26

Sly was such a cute colt. Unfortunately, his legs were developing crooked. He was extremely cow hocked. Cow-hocked is a conformation defect where the horse's hocks are too close together and their feet too far apart. The hock is basically the knee of the hind leg. Looking at a cow-hocked horse from the rear, his legs from hocks to hooves resemble an upside down V. By the time he was seven months old, our farrier said he thought we should "put him down" before we got too attached. Seriously!?!

I helped deliver this beautiful foal! I had been loving and training this delightful, flashy Appy colt for seven months. I think it was little late for "not too attached."

There was an excellent Equine Veterinarian located about two hours west of Pocatello. Many owners and trainers from California and other neighboring states would haul their valuable race and show horses all the way to Idaho for Dr Rupert to work his magic. He specialized in horses, specifically legs and lameness issues. We hauled Sly the 120 miles for the specialist to determine if there was some way to straighten his crooked legs.

Dr. Rupert told us it would actually be a pretty easy surgery. He would insert screws on the inside of his hocks to slow down growth there. He'd then make a small incision on the outside of each hock to promote development and allow the muscles and tendons to stretch and recover as the hock straightened. Sly was still a stud colt so the Vet offered to geld him while he was under anesthesia. It is normal to wait until a colt is at least a yearling or two-year-old to castrate them, but the doctor assured us that gelding him this young would have no ill effects on him. He actually wouldn't have to go through that naughty stage. (The stage when a colt, just like an adolescent boy, thinks he is a man, but is still really just an ill-behaved and mischievous bigger boy!)

The surgery was a success. Incredibly, our bill was less than $800.00! When I picked him up from the Equine Hospital a few days later, the surgeon was very pleased with Sly's progress. Sly was a trooper and had come through his ordeal with flying colors. He had behaved himself very well while at the clinic and the doctor and his staff were impressed with Sly's good manners. Happily, he was ready to come home and rejoin the family.

Sly continued to grow and his legs seemed to be developing properly now. He loved being handled and groomed. He learned to be patient with children, accepting of pressure and calm in the midst of tractors, dogs and 4-wheelers. He was turning into quite an all-around, dependable horse.

Sly, like all of my horses that I'd had since they were colts, was easy to train to be ridden. There was never any bucking or silliness. He was a good student and carried himself with confidence. Ears up, eyes bright, neck with a lovely arch, he was just a love.

Jennifer and her best friend, Angie, Casey's oldest daughter, decided they were finished with 4-H and wanted to join a riding club.   The group the girls wanted to join was called the Chaparrals and it was a family club. They were similar to the Silver Sage women's riding club that I was in when I was younger. Jennifer rode Sly and talked me into joining with her and riding Chachi. He was kind of a ringer in the speed events, but in fact, there were many exceptionally talented horses in the club.

There was one other Appaloosa in the group so Sly was partnered with him.   That little Appy, named Honcho, had been trained to bow.   The drill leader worked a bow into the drill. While Honcho was bowing, Sly and Jennifer were just supposed to stand by and wait for him. I guess Sly didn't like being upstaged, so while Honcho was bowing, Sly reared up on his hind legs. It was not planned but I think the crowd thought it was part of the act. It did look pretty cool . . . one handsome bay Appy bowing and a striking black Appy rearing. Jennifer handled it well, as she was a very good rider. The audience may have liked it, but Jennifer was incensed when she came out of the arena. I didn't blame her for being upset. There is nothing quite as frightening as a horse rearing when you didn't ask him to. Luckily, that was the only time he pulled that little stunt. If he'd started rearing as a reaction whenever he was nervous or under pressure, there's no telling how long it may have taken to get him to stop the perilous behavior. Sadly, many horses have been put down because of a dangerous rearing habit.

We had many fun times with Casey and his family. As I mentioned, Jennifer and Angie, were best friends and his two boys and TJ were about the same age and had lots of fun together. Lisa and Zack, the youngest of each family were great buddies too.

We all went on a trail ride over by Mackay, Idaho to a place called Copper Canyon. The mountains are breathtaking in that part of Idaho. The hillsides are thick with big and very fragrant Colorado blue and green spruce trees. The wildflowers are truly wild, and in great abundance and the sky seems to always be bright blue in the summertime. We'd ridden in about six miles on a fairly easy trail and had taken a break by a serene mountain lake. We rested ourselves and our horses, let the kids run around and be kids and had some lunch.

After lunch, Casey, Angie and the boys headed down the trail first. Rocke and Suzanne, Casey's wife had opted to hike rather than ride and Jennifer and I were bringing up the rear on Chachi and Sly. Zack was only four years old so he was riding behind my saddle on Chachi. We needed to cross a fairly wide creek. It was too wide to jump across so the experienced horses just waded through. On the way over the first time, Sly was a little hesitant, but eventually was persuaded to follow the other horses through. On the way back however, instead of calmly following Chachi through the creek, he decided he could jump across rather than wade. After his giant leap, he must have realized mid-air that he wasn't going to make it all the way. He saw a boulder off to the side and for a reason, only known to this three-year-old Appy, he adjusted course and landed spread eagle on the boulder.

Jennifer was thrown off and landed on the rocks in the creek. Sly scrambled off the boulder and up the side of the mountain just below the trail. Jennifer was in the creek wet and in pain and her thigh started swelling immediately. I jumped off and got Zack safely to the ground. I yelled for Casey and Rocke to come back. Rocke got to Jennifer and helped her out of the water so he could assess how badly she was hurt. The bruise forming on her thigh was massive. We were worried she may have fractured her leg. We decided the best thing we could do was get her down the trail as quickly as possible.

I left Casey with Chachi and Zack and slid down the side hill where Sly had ended up. My stomach was in knots. I was so afraid of what horrendous wounds I might find. He was pretty scraped up and had lost a shoe, but, thankfully, there were no broken legs or other serious injuries to him.

We helped Jennifer up on Chachi and started down the trail. I was leading Sly because I wanted to make it as easy on him as possible and be sure he wasn't lame. After about 20 minutes of him prancing and jigging down the trail, I figured if he was healthy and energetic enough to act up, I could ride him down.

Jennifer's leg healed without any complications. Sly's scrapes got better. *And* we had another exciting story to tell! It seemed whenever the Price and Acree families got together, it turned into an extreme adventure.

BAILE-1992

Chapter 27

Baile in 2005 in Texas

During the years that I was an honorary Price, (Chad often introduced me as his other daughter) he and I partnered on a horse on a few occasions. He would give me a young horse to train and I would work with it for a few months or sometimes, even a year or so. When he sold the horse we would split the profit.

One such joint venture brought me my next horse, Baile.

Her registered name was PF Miss Drew. PF stood for Price Farms. I don't know why they called it Price Farms. I thought farms produced crops and ranches raised horses and livestock. I always thought it should have been called Price Ranch, but that was just me. As the years passed, it did evolve into being called the Ranch.

I had gone to the field where Chad said there were two yearlings and I could choose one to take home and train. Both horses were mares and something about the mousy brown filly made me choose her. I imagine it was her gorgeous eyes and petite, sculptured head.

I got her in the trailer without much fuss, but as I started to drive out, the trailer started rocking and there was a lot of loud banging. I jumped out of the truck and ran back to the horse trailer only to find that the filly had thrown herself on the floor of the trailer and was stuck.

I was still using my little old two-horse trailer and unfortunately the center divider was not moveable. So, with some tugging and pushing and a lot of sweat, I got her back to her feet. She was already scraped up and I hadn't even driven out of the pasture yet!

When I got her home, I started calling her Mouse. I thought it was kind of cute. I tried Missy and Drew, but they just didn't fit this quiet beauty. My mom came over to see the newest addition to our herd. I told her I was going to name her Mouse and she said, "Ooh, that's an awful name!"

Hmmm, I thought it was a perfectly fine name, but I started trying out other names anyway. While I was in the barn grooming her one day, I muttered, "What color are you?" "Coffee...but that doesn't seem quite right for a name." "What goes with coffee? Cream, sugar? Ahh, my favorite, Bailey's Irish Cream!" So, Baile it was; Baile with an 'e.'

Rocke had started the tradition of leaving the 'y' off the end of our pets' names. His mom had done it when she named him Rocke, with an 'e.' When we got married he had a lovable golden retriever named Brande, we had to call her Brande Dog, since I also had Brandey Horse at the time.

TJ riding Brandey Horse with Brande Dog close behind

I started Baile's ground training as soon as I got her settled in. She was one of the easiest horses I've ever trained.   She was an early foal.   Her birthday was February 24, so she was strong enough to start lightly under saddle the winter before she even turned two.

By mid-summer, I was able to ride her down the road or in the arena. She was dependable no matter where I took her. She was trustworthy with the kids and a good pasture mate to my other horses.

Baile's only small negative issues were with injections and fly spray. She didn't throw a big fit over either, but she always flinched when getting her annual vaccinations and the first time I sprayed her with fly spray, she let out a moan like I had just kicked her hard in the gut. She still doesn't love fly spray and every once in a while will let out a little "Ugh!" when I spray her belly.

When she was just two, I took her on a camping trail ride with some girlfriends. They had older, more experienced horses that had a bad habit or two. All they could talk about the whole weekend was how amazingly good my filly was being.

One day while I was visiting with Chad, he asked. "How's our horse coming along?" I replied, "Oh Chad, she is such a great little horse, I might just have to buy her from you." He said, in his Papa Chad way, "Ah hell, you have more into her now than I do. I'll just give her to ya." And he did; registration papers and all. I was so fortunate to have this wonderful, generous man be such a big part of my life.

Her four-year-old year, I started to introduce her to barrels and poles. We just walked the patterns so she would get the idea. She was pretty fast, as she had been bred to race. She was registered as an Appendix Quarter Horse, which simply meant that one of her parents was a Thoroughbred and one was Quarter Horse. In her case, her dam was the Thoroughbred. She grew to be about 15 hands. Not too tall and not too small, she was a perfect size.

I continued riding and training Baile as a five-year-old. Even though she was bred to be a race horse, she was always a little bit stumbley. I was running her on the poles, just practicing in my arena, when she slipped and fell down. We were in a sharp turn at the end pole, and as she slid down on one side, she pinned my leg underneath her. Having a 1000-pound horse on your leg is not pleasant. When she finally regained her feet and I was able to step off, I was hurting. No one else was home. Luckily, my uncle just happened to drive up as I was hobbling and moaning on my way out of the arena and to the barn. He helped me get Baile put away after giving her a quick once over to make sure she hadn't injured herself and he took me to the house and we assessed my damages. Nothing was broken or bleeding, but man did I have an awesome, colorful bruise the entire length of my leg.

I was beginning to question whether Baile had the athleticism to be a speed event horse.

Chapter 28

I sold Brandey in 1991. He was 18 years old and Jennifer was no longer using him in 4-H and Zack was only five at that time, and not quite ready for a horse of his own. I was busy with Chachi and Sly as well as several outside horses I had in training. Brandey just wasn't being ridden enough. I felt he still had a lot to offer as a 4-H horse, so I came to the very difficult decision to sell him. He went to a family with children in 4-H and I was comfortable that he would be going to a good and caring home.

In 1994, when Zack was eight years old and almost 4-H age, we decided to buy him an experienced 4-H horse. At this time, Baile was only two and I was just starting her training.

Zack had tried some of the sports that TJ loved so much, but he just didn't care for team competition. He did however, have a passion for horses, just like his big sister. He had no fear and was very confident around them.

We'd watched a family use a big bright sorrel roan horse for a few years and they had been very successful in the show ring with him. Come to find out, they had originally bought him from Chad. The horse had been born with a foot defect and had to have three pins surgically placed in his pastern. The pastern is the area just below the horse's ankle and above the hoof line.

The family was aware the horse had the pins, but after using him for several years for horse shows, they decided to make him a barrel horse for their daughters.

With the pins in his foot, he was not going to hold up to the pounding that running barrels creates. Chad, being the kind of man he is and even though he had no obligation to do so, bought the horse back from them. What they really wanted was some cash to buy another horse. I'm sure Karma has caught up with them by now.

I'd watched the horse perform, and thought he would be a great first horse for Zack. Chad had given him the nickname John Wayne. He was big and stout and had lots of chrome. By chrome, I mean he had a wide white blaze on his face, four bright white stockings and a raccoon striped tail. He was a very classy looking horse.

Qually in 1995

His registered name was He Qualified. His last family had called him Qually. Since that's what he answered to when we called him from the pasture, we stuck with it. Zack loved Qually and spoiled him with an occasional treat of Froot Loops. Qually was very gentle and they got along great. Zack was only eight, so he looked pretty little up there. Qually was at least 16½ hands. The fact that he was so big didn't bother Zack at all. He was comfortable on horses and rode very well from the beginning.

Right after we bought Qually in early spring, Casey asked me to come to the ranch and ride a young race filly that he was training. She'd been entered into a stallion incentive futurity as soon as she was born. The owners of some race horses will oftentimes do this if they believe a colt is going to be particularly talented. He had expressed to the owners that she was awfully small to be starting race training but they insisted that he continue with her training anyway.

This young mare was very small boned as a two-year old and Casey was concerned that he was too heavy for her. While I worked the little filly, he was going to ride another colt he had in training. Since we were going to the ranch, Zack wanted to take Qually and ride around while we worked the colts in the arena.

We saddled the colts and Qually at the hitching posts up by the barns. Casey told me he had ridden the filly at least ten times, but she still acted up every time he threw his leg over her back and into the stirrup on the other side. So, as I was swinging into the saddle, I was mindful of that issue. She skittered away from me as I started to get on her, but once my leg was over her back, she settled down.

Casey and Zack got on their horses and we headed down the lane to the arena. They had built it in the front section of the lower pasture that was behind Chad's house. They had only plowed and harrowed a portion of the fenced area.

Once in the arena, I started by working the filly at a walk. Then we trotted and practiced stopping and turning to the pressure from the bit. She was going nicely, so I started to canter her around the perimeter of the tilled area of the arena. By this time, we had been riding for about twenty minutes. Casey's colt seemed to be working well also. He was bigger and more stoutly built than the filly and was also being trained for the track. We had gone about halfway around the arena when, all of a sudden, she just took off bucking. She didn't stop and buck in place; instead she bucked and ran, increasing her speed with every jump. On the second or third hard buck, she yanked the reins out my hands. Now, we were heading straight for the arena fence and I had no reins. I decided the prudent thing to do, would be to get off! I jumped from the saddle and landed on my feet and hands. Picture a gymnast landing a terrific vault and then throwing her arms in the air in triumph of not falling back. I didn't throw my hands up but, I lingered in the bent over position for a few beats to regain my balance. As I stood up, I was thinking, Wow! That was a pretty good landing!

Casey trotted over on his colt and asked "Why'd ya get off?" I told him I'd lost the reins and figured I had no other reasonable choice! We couldn't figure out what had set off the little mare; probably nothing more than the fact that she was still so green (meaning she was about in the kindergarten stage of her schooling.) He asked if I was okay. I said I thought so, but my wrists hurt a little from breaking the fall with my hands. The filly had bucked over to the area of the arena that had not been tilled up. The ground was very hard as it was early spring and still quite cold out.

We decided to trade colts for a while to see if he could work the bucks out of the filly. As I raised my left hand to take hold of the reins on the big colt, a shooting pain streaked down my wrist. I said "Ow! Wait a minute Casey, I better take a look." When I took off my glove, it was apparent I had probably broken my wrist. It had already started to swell and turn purple. The more I moved it, the more excruciating the pain was. I guess the training session was over; I needed to go get my wrist checked out at the hospital emergency room.

Casey helped Zack get Qually unsaddled and loaded into our trailer. He hurriedly put the colts away and then followed us home. I drove with my hurt arm resting in my lap, trying not to move it. When we got home, Casey and Zack put Qually away and unhooked the truck from the horse trailer. While they did that, I went to the house to call my mom to see if she could come over and take me to the hospital. She said she'd be right over. Casey waited with me until she got there. He felt like it was his fault that I'd gotten hurt, but it was not. I should've been more attentive while riding such a volatile young horse. I guess it was my turn to have a broken bone as a result of a Casey and Susan adventure.

Mom and I were just about to pull in to the ER entrance when Rocke passed us going the other way on the road as he was on his way home from work. His office was just down the street from the hospital. We waved him down and he followed us into the hospital parking lot. Mom handed me off to Rocke and then went home to watch the boys for us until we got back.

After reading my x-rays, the ER Doctor told us my wrist was, in fact, broken. He said the good news was the bone was not displaced, so it would not need to be reset. Yea! That *was* good news! My arm was too swollen to cast right then, so he told me to make an appointment with an orthopedic surgeon for later in the week to get it casted. He wrapped my wrist in a splint and put me in a sling to support my arm in the interim.

At the end of the week, I went to the orthopedic specialist to get my wrist casted. He took new x-rays and came back in the room to tell me the bad news. The bone *was* displaced and now, since it had been five days since the injury, he would have to re-break and set the broken bone. Ooh! That *was* bad news! It sounded way too painful to me.

The doctor had me lay back on the examination bed. He injected a local anesthesia at the break site. "Ouch!" is an understatement. There is not much soft tissue on the wrist so it felt like he stuck the needle straight into the bone.

After allowing my wrist to become numb, he picked up my arm and just held it with both hands, slowly massaging the break site with his thumbs. "Snap!" I felt like I my whole body came up off the table in pain. "Aggghhhh! That really, really hurt!" The doctor continued to rub my wrist softly with warm hands. The pain started to subside a bit. He apologized and said that the numbing medicine actually took away about 90% of the pain. I told him if I ever had to have that done again, I would *not* give him my hand so willingly. He would have to knock me out to take away 100% of the pain.

I chose dark purple for my cast color. I knew with my country lifestyle it was bound to get dirty. Even though the break was in my wrist, the cast engulfed my entire arm. I was bright purple from armpit to thumb. The doctor warned me that any impact on the back of my elbow could easily cause my wrist to snap again. He was pretty adamant that I not ride for the next six weeks. What? I couldn't stand that! I conceded that I probably couldn't swing a saddle up on a horse's back. I also agreed to no barrel racing or pole bending, but insisted that riding around the arena and pasture bareback should be okay.

Chapter 29

When Zack was nine, he started 4-H with Qually. That July, I took Zack and Qually to 4-H horse camp in Alpine, Wyoming. I'd borrowed some panels from a friend to build a portable corral at the back of our trailer. Without panels, the horses at camp were expected to stay tied to the trailers all night. I thought that was a lot to ask of Qually, so he got the luxury of a small corral. At least he could move around a bit and lie down if he wanted to.

The camp was made up of boys and girls cabins, located on opposite sides of the lodge. The lodge was a massive log structure with a great room in the front and a huge rock fireplace at one end; the room doubled as the dining hall. At the back of the building was a very large kitchen area. They served breakfast, lunch and dinner. During the days, some of the classes were held in the lodge. In the evenings there would be social gatherings such as talent shows and karaoke in the great room. On the last night of camp, there was the much anticipated dance.

Zack stayed in one of the boy's cabins. This was a little intimidating for him, as he was the only one from his 4-H club to go to horse camp that year. He didn't know anyone the first day, but by the second, he had a bunch of new friends. He has stayed in touch with many of the friends he met during his 4-H years.

I just slept in the back of the truck. I preferred that because I was right next to the horses, although, it was a bit noisy with all of the horses talking back and forth all night. They were worse than teenagers!

Each day at camp consisted of classes and workshops for the 4-Hers. Parents and leaders were also invited to take part. Many of the classes were held in the post and pole arenas that had been built in the meadows surrounding the camp. They weren't tilled or even mowed, so the horses had to go over or around sagebrush bushes and wildflowers. Other classes were held wherever the presenter could find a spot to set up.

One of our favorite non-horse activities was the rope braiding. An older cowboy set up his class under giant pine trees that encircled a small flat area. He had several spools of brightly colored nylon cord. He also handed out leaflets that showed the different knots and braids that we could use on our projects. We could tie rope halters and braid lead ropes, reins and even dog collars and leashes. He would give a demonstration, then, wander from student to student helping get everyone started and then fixing the endless mistakes that each of us made. He had infinite patience. Zack and I still have many sets of reins and a couple of rope halters from horse camp.

It was always a great experience to spend one-on-one time with my children. When Jennifer and Angie were in 4-H, I took them to Alpine also. We always had so much fun and made such wonderful memories. One night, when the girls and I were at camp, a parent angrily knocked on our cabin door. There were five girls plus me in the cabin. I opened the door and she scolded "You need to settle down in there, you're being too noisy! Who is the adult here?" I said "I am! I thought we were here to allow our children to have fun. All of my girls are in the cabin, not breaking any rules, and just learning a new dance, lighten up!" I guess I wasn't the typical chaperone. Thank goodness!

Zack went to practices up at the fairgrounds, just as Jennifer had a few years earlier, and, as I had done so many years ago. Unfortunately, Qually came up lame just a couple of weeks before fair time. We were trying to figure out what to do so Zack could finish the year and show in the County Fair at the end of the summer.

Just by chance, I was at the grocery store and ran into an old friend. Jennifer had been in 4-H with his daughter. I was telling him about Qually and he said. "Why don't you use Magic?" Magic was his daughter, Sara's horse. She had used her in 4-H and had been extremely successful. Sara was no longer in 4-H and had moved on to Junior Rodeo. He told me that Magic was just standing out in the pasture getting fat and it would be good for her to be used.

I was a little hesitant. I didn't really like to borrow or lend horses. Too much can go wrong. He assured me it'd be fine and I arranged to pick her up for Zack's next practice.

She was so experienced and such a steady horse, Zack immediately felt comfortable on her. He continued to practice for the fair with Magic and was looking forward to his first horse show.

Chapter 30

At this time in our lives, we were all struggling with the fact that my dad was suffering from cancer. It was August, 1995. He'd been bald most of his life and developed a Melanoma mole on his head. The doctor noticed the tiny mole on a routine check-up. He was immediately scheduled for surgery to remove the mole. Melanoma is a nasty type of cancer. The specialists told us by the time you can see the mole, it is usually too late. The cancer spreads to the vital organs of the body. This was the same type of cancer that killed James five years earlier. It seemed our lives were still running on parallel paths, but this time in a devastating way.

It was so unfair. My wonderful, gentle, kind father was going to die. He was not going to see his grandchildren grow into adults. He was going to miss horse shows and football games, graduations and weddings. We were all distraught. A second opinion resulted in the same news being given, just by a different, more compassionate doctor.

By the time the fair rolled around, we'd all come to some sort of grip of the fact my dad was terminal. He was now bedridden and my mom had become his full time caregiver. We were trying to keep life as normal as possible for our children, but they too felt the very real weight of the loss we had already started to experience.

Mom had made arrangements for someone to come to the house and stay with Dad while she came up to watch Zack in his classes. He was scheduled to show in his first class with Magic right after lunch.

The morning classes ended up having a small number of participants, so they finished up very quickly. The announcer told us over the loud speaker that all of the classes had been moved to an earlier start time. At the fair, we always camped at the lower part of the fairgrounds. Zack and I rushed down to the camp trailer so he could get his show clothes on and his number pinned to his back for his first class.

He had his bike, so he took off for the barn. He said he would get Magic out of her stall and start brushing her. I told him I needed to stop at the payphone to call Grandma to let her know that his classes were starting early. I was hoping she could still make it up to watch.

I ran from the payphone that was located under the grandstands just south of the barn where the 4-H horses were stalled. They'd really put the rush on everybody by changing the class times. The barn area was bustling with hurried pre-class activity.

I came around the corner of the barn to the most horrific sight I have ever witnessed. Magic was on her side, her head lifted off the ground by the lead rope tied to the hitching post. Her belly had been slit from between her front legs all the way to her hind legs.

All I could think after seeing the horror of the scene was "where's Zack?" Our 4-H leader was there as well as many other parents and children. Someone had pushed Zack behind a nearby car as soon as the accident happened. I grabbed him and ran farther away. I went behind our horse trailer and held Zack close to me. He was crying and asked what was happening. Our leader found us and told us that Magic had to be put down, she was struggling, the rope broke and her insides were spilling out. I cried "She's not my horse!" He said there was nothing that could be done. I had to make the decision. I sheltered Zack's ears and sobbed "Shoot her, put her out of her misery!" He ran back to the mayhem. Men were holding Magic down to keep her from struggling any more. Our 4-H leader's wife had a handgun in her purse. Because they lived on the nearby Indian Reservation, she felt she needed it for safety. I was so thankful she had that gun.

Zack heard the gunshot. He flinched and cried "What was that?" I had no choice but to tell him the awful truth... that Magic had to be put down.

I felt horrible. I had sheltered Zack from the horror, but many of the other 4-Hers were right there; seeing something that even adults should never have to see, ever. I ran away with my child while everyone else was dealing with the gruesome scene. They quickly covered Magic's body with a blanket and parents ushered their children away to try to calm them and explain the tragedy.

As I was trying to get Zack back to the camp trailer, Magic's teenage owner, Sara drove into the parking lot. She saw us and stopped. She got out of the car with a smile, so excited to watch her sweet horse and Zack. When she saw my face, contorted with grief, she hugged me and asked. "What's wrong?" Through tears and sobs I choked out that Magic was dead. She was dumbstruck. She could not believe what I had just told her. She started to walk back to the barn area and I implored her not to go. She absolutely could not see Magic. Sara helped me call her dad at work to relay the horrible news.

That day is still a blur. As I recount the ghastly event for this writing, my heart is pounding, my stomach is tight and stinging tears are hard to hold back.

Eventually, Rocke and, TJ, Mom and Jennifer came to the fairgrounds to try to comfort us and take us home. What had started out to be such a day of excitement and joy for Zack had turned into a nightmare...*literally*. He and I would suffer from the effects of Magic's death for a long, long time.

As I tried to piece together what had actually happened that fateful morning, I came up with this account.

Zack had brought Magic out of her stall and tied her to the hitching post/wash rack. The fairgrounds maintenance men had added hose spigots to the hitching rail where the kids tied their horses. At the time, it seemed like a great idea. Previously, there had been only one wash bay and the 4-Hers would have to stand and wait in line to wash their horses. With this new wash bay, three or four horses could get their baths at the same time.

The problem was the design. Hose spigots had been welded to the top of the rail; they should have been attached underneath. On one end of the rail, the valve handle had been broken causing a jagged, sharp edge.

From the details I'd heard, something had spooked Magic. This was very hard to imagine because I'd never seen her pull back while tied. And, she was not easily frightened. When she pulled back from the rail and her lead rope tightened, she lunged forward and landed on the broken water valve. As she slid back off, the sharp metal acted as a scalpel and sliced her belly open.

The fair went on that year with heavy hearts. Of course, Zack wasn't able to take part in any of his classes. However, after we went home for a while to calm down and get cleaned up, we convinced him we should stay up at the fairgrounds and take part in the other activities to help get his mind off the tragedy with Magic.

It helped a bit. His group even awarded him a blue ribbon for sportsmanship so he wouldn't go home without a ribbon. Although, he appreciated the gesture, I don't think he cared about a ribbon.

I felt so awful for Magic's owners. No one could ever have foreseen such a dreadful outcome from simply borrowing a nice 4-H horse. I made Sara a little plaque out of Magic's name plate that Zack had made to decorate her stall at the fair. I told Sara's dad I would pay him for Magic or give him Baile. He refused. He said it was a tragic accident and he didn't blame me or Zack.

He was all too familiar with tragedy. A year or two earlier, he'd taken Sara and her best friend on a camping trip. On the highway, he lost control of the truck and camp trailer which resulted in a horrible wreck. Sara's best friend was killed. Sara had suffered a broken leg and other severe injuries. Her dad had been in a coma since the accident. When he woke up, his family told him the dreadful news of the death of Sara's friend. He never really recovered from that accident, physically or emotionally. That day as I sat crying at his kitchen table, he said, "Susan, you didn't bring back a horse. I didn't bring back someone's child."

After Magic died and remembering her best friend, Sara asked her dad "Why does everything I love die?" I don't know what his answer was, but I knew I was so sorry that I'd caused her even more pain and grief in her young life.

A couple of years later, I was able to give back, a little, to Sara. In 1997, she was competing in high school rodeo and really didn't have a top notch horse. I let her use Chachi. I finally upgraded from my little old two horse trailer in 1996. We had a custom three horse slant load trailer built to our specifications, just as my folks had done 30+ years earlier. That little old trailer served me well for more than 20 years. I would load up Chachi in my new horse trailer and then go pick up Sara and take her to the high school rodeos.

Sara did well, but didn't have the kind of year she was hoping for. She didn't make it to the State High

School Rodeo Finals, although, I think when she first started running Chachi; she thought she might have a chance. Even so, I hope she enjoyed having me go to those high school rodeos with her as much as I enjoyed taking her. I loved watching Sara ride Chachi. It's not often you get a chance to see your own horse compete. Until then, I had only viewed his barrel runs from atop his back.

I am happy that Sara and I remain friends today and she now has her own little cowboy.

Chapter 31

My dad passed away on September 3, 1995. He was only 61 years old. I remember the day Mom called us over, saying his time was getting close. I held his hand, said my goodbye and cried with my cheek on his chest. Then, he let out one last breath and was gone.

Jennifer had already gone back to Oregon for her senior year of high school. When she left, she knew she would never see her Grandpa again. They had a special relationship and shared a passion for chocolate Ding Dongs. My dad always made sure he had her favorite chocolate treats in the freezer when Jennifer visited.

TJ was thirteen and Zack was only nine. We left them at home when we went to see Dad that last time. Hours later, after we finally got back home, we sat in our living room and told them that Grandpa had passed away. We were worried about Zack, he and my dad had become especially close that last year. But it was TJ, who, although he was trying his best not to cry, had a wobbly chin and just could not hold back tears that slowly streamed down his cheeks.

My dad had lived his life well. Everyone loved him. Friends, family and mere acquaintances all had stories of the kindness of my father. His quiet wit, his incredible thoughtfulness, his amazing talent as a woodworker and his gentle way, would be missed dearly by all who knew and loved him. There was a very big hole in our lives now.

Zack started fourth grade that fall and seemed to be getting along okay. We did tell the school counselor of the accident and about the loss of his grandfather. She had a few sessions with Zack to make sure he wasn't bottling up his grief.

I, on the other hand was not coping well. I was so sad about losing my dad that I hadn't resolved or emotionally dealt with Magic's accident. I would be driving down the road and burst out crying. I just could not get the appalling vision out of my head. I couldn't sleep without seeing the gore. Anytime I had empty time, there it was again. I finally decided I needed to get some counseling.

I found a psychologist and scheduled an appointment. I'd never experienced therapy so I didn't know what to expect. I did know something had to change or I was going to drive myself mad with the images of that catastrophic day.

On my first visit, I relived the horror of that day...all of it, every gruesome detail. I also told her about my dad and how worried I was about Zack. She told me about a rapid eye movement therapy that had been successful in treating soldiers who suffered from PTSD, Post-Traumatic Stress Disorder. These military people had seen ghastly things in war and those scenes haunted them when they returned home. She also told me, they, the psychology world, didn't know exactly why it worked, it just did. I was willing to give almost anything a try.

First, she had me think of the grisly scene and work myself back up to a high level of anxiety, tears and all. Then, she would move a pencil back and forth like a pendulum and have me watch it, back and forth, back and forth. She was not hypnotizing me, but with every swing, my anxiety would lessen just a bit. She would do this, two or three times per session. I finally started to see some results and felt myself healing. I'll be forever grateful to her and to Zack's school counselor for helping us get through that awful time.

I still miss Dad every day. But even though I didn't have him nearly long enough, at least I had him. He taught by example. My children, even as young as they were when we lost him, remember his subtle lessons. When any of them are at a moral crossroad, they think, "What would Grandpa do?"

Race was my shoulder to cry on when I was down. Earlier in the year, May of 2006, we had to have my precious German Shorthaired Pointer, Murphe, put down. She was nearly 15 years old and her body had just worn out. Our Vet came to the house to put her to sleep. I tried to be strong and stay with her, but I just couldn't. I felt that my being so upset would be harder on Murphe than if I just walked away. So, I left Rocke with her to hold her as she took her last breath, and I went to the barn, to Race. I put his halter on and had him sidle up to the fence so I could get on bareback. We walked out to farthest corner of the pasture that overlooked the cattle ranch across the road. I cried and sobbed until there was nothing left. And Race, he stood stoic, he never moved a muscle, he just absorbed it all....

After he died, I found myself wanting to go to the barn for comfort -- from Race -- but he wasn't there. Only Baile was there, and she was just as brokenhearted as I was.....

Chapter 32

The next year Zack went back to riding Qually for 4-H. His lameness had resolved itself with some time off. But evidently, Qually liked his life of luxury as a pasture ornament. Every time Zack would ride Qually, he would kick up if asked to gallop. I started having to warm him up to get the kicks out, before Zack got on.

On one particularly unforgettable day, I was cantering Qually around the arena, thinking that all of his kick-ups had been exhausted, when all of a sudden I was flying through the air. He had launched me over his head. My only decision was which way to tuck and roll.

Zack and Qually winning First Place

Zack showed him at the fair that year, the first day went great, he and Qually won first place in the Western Equitation Class. He rode so well...he put Qually on the correct lead in both directions, his transitions were flawless and he had a perfect, straight and smooth back-up.

The next day started with me getting up early to take Qually to the warm up arena, in hopes of another non-eventful class for Zack. It didn't work this time. The first time the judge called for the canter, Qually kicked up. Zack was fine and was just going to canter on, but the announcer panicked and said "Stop. Everyone stop your horses!" The judge then instructed Zack to canter around the ring by himself rather than with the rest of the nine and ten-year-old riders. He didn't want to risk Qually kicking another horse...or worse a child. Better safe than sorry. Nobody wanted any drama or trauma this year at the fair.

Since Qually obviously thought his showing days should be over, we sold him to a neighbor down the road. She just wanted a horse she could ride on the canal banks and along the edges of the hay fields. This would be the nice easy life Qually evidently felt he had earned. When I first started talking about selling Qually, Zack was not willing to even discuss it. But after the last incident at the fair, he was so irritated with him, he agreed it might be time to move on to Baile.

Zack also got to use the money we received from the sale of Qually to buy a little 4-wheeler. That made it a little easier to say goodbye, and Qually was just a few houses away if he wanted to visit him.

As soon as Zack could reach the gas pedal and brake in the truck, he started hooking up the trailer before 4-H practice and then he would back it in to the parking spot and unhitch it when we got home.

Zack was always the mechanic and electronics guru of the family. If anything ever needed fixing, we all--Rocke and I, TJ and Jennifer, grandparents, neighbors and even the teachers at the elementary school-- would ask for Zack's assistance and expertise in making the needed repairs and connections.

I remember one day coming home to find his little 4-wheeler taken completely apart with parts strewn all over the garage floor. Rocke got home, took one look at the mess and calmly said "Put. It. Back. Together." Zack was only ten years old at the time. He did get it all back together, with only a couple of parts left over, but it still started and ran just fine. We were pretty impressed, but we had to act stern.

With Qually's exit from the herd, I stopped Baile's barrel training and informed her that she was now a   4-H horse. This fit her level of athletic ability much better and she and Zack had many good years together in 4-H and team penning. They developed a close and special bond. She is now 21 years old and whenever he visits, she perks up, nickers a "Hello" and trots up to the gate to greet him. All he has to do is whistle and call her name. He has always called her BaileMae.

Zack and Baile competing in Team Penning in 1997

She is now the resident *good old horse,* just like Happy Appy was all those years ago. Zack's two children as well as our other grandchildren just love Baile. They spoil her with hugs and treats of which she is absolutely and totally deserving.

RACE-1993

Chapter 33

Race at six months, with Murphe in the background
He was stunning, even as a baby.

He looked a lot like Chachi, dark chestnut with a flaxen mane and fluffy foal tail. Chad and I were out looking over the new crop of foals and I told him "If I could pick one, I would want him," pointing out the cute liver chestnut colt with the perfect blaze and two white socks on his hind legs. He told me I couldn't have him because he was out of his Merridoc mare and he was "Gonna be a good one." I told him then, that Racing On By was the only colt in the field for me.

Even though at first, Chad said the handsome colt wasn't for sale, I knew Chad; everything on his place is ultimately for sale. So, with a little persistence, he gave me a price. Wow, that was a lot for a six-month-old colt. I actually wasn't even looking for another horse; Race just caught my eye and my heart in that first instant. At the time, I had Chachi, who was ten years old and still going strong as my barrel and pole bending horse.

We also had Sly, but since he was not going to have the athleticism for the type of riding I wanted to do, I decided it was time to find him a home where he could be a good saddle horse, but not have his legs stressed too much physically. I put an ad in the paper and priced him at $2000.00. Rocke asked me how much I wanted for him and I said $2000.00. He encouraged me to change the price in the ad to $2500.00, then, I would have some bargaining room.

The first man to look at him liked him immediately. He was such a nice-looking horse, with a sweet face and kind eye; traits that are sometimes hard to come by in Appaloosas. He rode him for a while then asked me if he had ever had a rope swung on him, I said no, but he could give it a try. It was immediately apparent that this guy was a ranch roper not a rodeo roper, he fumbled around with his rope for a bit, and Sly was just as good as gold, standing patiently while the new guy on his back swung the rope all around him and over his head. The buyer was impressed.

When I realized that he really liked Sly and was very interested in him, I told him about the surgery he'd had on his hind legs when he was a colt. I believe in full disclosure when selling a horse. He asked me if I would guarantee his legs and I said I would as much as the Veterinarian had guaranteed them to me. He told me that he'd performed the same surgery on some race horses and that they were still racing. That was good enough for him and he asked me if I would take $2250.00 for him. I said yes, *since* I thought he would be going to a good home. The man just needed a horse to work his cattle ranch and for his kids to ride every once in a while. He felt he was getting a bonus because Sly was such an attractive horse.

I asked if he wanted me to load Sly and follow him home rather than him having to come all the way back to get him. He said "Sure, if you don't mind and have the time." Just one more thing to impress him; Sly just hopped into the trailer and off we went. It took about an hour to get to his place, and I was feeling pretty cheerless the whole way.

We pulled into his ranch and I unloaded Sly. His kids ran out to greet us and started hugging him with enthused attention. Then, they just walked him away from me; I can still remember the scene, of me standing sadly watching his beautiful, white blanketed rump slowly disappear into the fading evening light with excited, chattering children closely following alongside. I didn't even get to say goodbye to this sweet horse that I'd had since he'd hit the ground, literally. I held it together until I was back in the truck and on my way home, then, the flood gates opened and I wept all the way home.

I've never been able to sell horses very easily; they're part of my family. I was sitting at the kitchen table feeling really blue when Rocke came in. He asked what was wrong and I told him I'd sold Sly. He perked up immediately, looked toward the pasture and asked if he was gone. Even though he always supported me in my horse fanaticism, he was always quick to say we had too many horses. Even so, after his initial delight that we had trimmed the herd down, he realized that I was pretty sad and asked "So, are you going to go get that colt?" Talk about perking up! I looked at him through red rimmed eyes that now had a "Really?" expression in them. He asked how much I got for Sly, and said it seemed like I could afford the colt now. What a wonderful man I married. I grabbed the checkbook and headed out to Chad's place.

Chapter 34

I bought Racing On By, aka Race, when he was five months old in 1993. He had megastar written all over him. He was a grandson of the greatest Quarter Horse Stallion of modern time, Dash For Cash, and looked almost identical to him.

Interestingly, Brandey was born in 1973 and was ten years old when Chachi was born. Chachi was born in 1983 and was ten years old when Race was born.

After buying Race, I anxiously awaited the time he would be old enough to wean so I could finally bring him home. A foal is usually weaned at about six months. I took my truck and little trailer to the ranch to pick him up. I still had the same little blue foal halter that I first used on Chachi and then later on Sly.

I walked through the lush green pasture towards Race and the other weanlings. They all watched my approach with bright eyes and pricked up ears. The colts were curious about me as a stranger occupying their domain. As I got a little closer, some of the colts started to get a little nervous and cautiously moved away. Not Race. He stood and waited for me to walk right up to him. He seemed to be saying with those beautiful, expressive eyes "Hello, I've been waiting for you. Let's go home."

He almost haltered himself, which is incredible for a colt so young. I held the halter open and he sought out the opening and eagerly stuck his nose through. I buckled it on his cute little head and just started leading him from the pasture. No tugging or pulling from me or him. As I reached the pasture gate, Chad was waiting for us and jokingly said "No extra charge for the halter training." We loaded him up with no fuss and we were on our way...to what would become a phenomenal and extraordinary relationship. We were destined to be horse to human soul mates.

I fell more in love with Race the moment I got him home. He settled into life at the Acree homestead quickly and easily. Chachi was the leader of the herd. Baile was just a yearling, so she had not yet taken on the role of Alpha Mare. In the wild, the stallion is the protector of the herd, but it is the Alpha Mare that makes the decisions for the whole herd. She decides when to move and when to rest, when and where to graze, and which way and how fast to travel. When Baile got some age and experience on her, she became our little herd's lead mare.

A few weeks after I got Race home, he somehow injured his shoulder. One morning before leaving for work, I went out to check on the horses and Race looked like maybe he'd been kicked or had some kind of puncture wound. I called the Veterinary Clinic that I'd always gone to, the one that was right across the road from my mom's place. They said they couldn't see him that day, as they were closing early. I was beyond irritated. He didn't seem to be lame and I was already late for work, so I decided to see how he was by the end of the day. When I got home, he seemed a little better. The next morning was a Saturday and when I went out to check on Race, his shoulder was worse. It'd started draining pus and a bloody discharge. I called the other equine clinic and they told me the doctor would be right over. That was all it took for me to switch Vet clinics, even after going to the one by my parent's place for more than two decades. When I have an emergency, I need to be treated with respect and urgency.

When Dr. Higgins arrived, he determined that he needed to examine and treat Race at the clinic, so he helped me load him up and followed me back to the clinic. Now that's customer service! I never regretted my decision to switch Vets. Doc Higgins and I have remained friends ever since that first early Saturday morning meeting. Race ended up having a small puncture wound in his shoulder, no other damage. I had to keep it clean and medicated while it healed from the inside out. It healed up nicely with no ill effects.

Unfortunately, I would soon realize that Race could probably get hurt in a padded stall!

While he was still a baby, he somehow cut his hind leg on the end of a 2 x 4 piece of lumber that was part of the hay manger in the barn. He must have stepped straight down on it and caught the edge just right to cause the injury. The edge wasn't even sharp, just a freak accident. His left rear leg appeared as if someone had taken a hunting knife to it. It looked like it had been skinned, with the hide of his lower leg just hanging around his hoof. It was a grisly sight. Back to the Vet clinic we go! Over twenty stitches and couple hundred dollars later, we were on our way back home. Again, Race healed well and had a scar that wrapped around his lower leg. It was hardly noticeable because the scar was right at the line between his chestnut brown upper leg and the top of his white stocking.

As for his training, I started him slow, made sure he had impeccable ground manners and that he was easy to handle in every-day situations. He was a love. When he was about 18 months old, I decided I should get him castrated (gelded), I didn't need a stud horse. Just before his appointment, I got news that his sire, Buy For Cash had suddenly died. I thought about keeping him a stud to continue the line, but thankfully, good sense returned and I went ahead and had him gelded. He was a good boy before, but after he was just amazing!

As Race continued to mature both physically and mentally, I continued with his training, with the ultimate goal that he would someday be a barrel racing Phenom.

One dreary January night in 1996, I heard a clattering. I lay in bed and listened intently. There it was again. I jumped up and looked out to see what it might be. Winter rain seems to cause the night to be absolutely pitch-black. As I strained to see through the rain out the back windows, I finally noticed that the arena gate was open. I hurriedly muttered, "Oh, shoot! The horses are out."

With a groan, Rocke groggily got out of bed to help me. We jumped into our winter boots, hurriedly threw on our coats and headed out to capture the escapees. When I got outside, I realized they'd run back into the arena. Whew! At least they weren't running down the road at midnight. I opened the corral gate and herded them back in. It was dark, rainy and miserable. Rocke had been fighting a cold, so he started to go back in the house. I said "Race looked like he's moving kind of weird, I'm going to double check him and make sure he's alright." Then, I told him to go ahead and go back to bed, I would be right in.

Race was standing out in the corral behind the barn. I could just make out his silhouette. He was standing calmly, but he had his right front leg propped up on the toe of his hoof. He was putting absolutely no weight on that leg.

I grabbed his halter and trudged out to bring him into the barn. I needed to look at him more closely in the light. I led him in with him limping behind me. He was hopping on his left front leg, still unwilling to place any weight on the injured right leg. Oh, what a horrid sight! There was a gaping gash around his entire knee joint. I could have fit my entire fist in the wound. A white tendon was dangling from the inside of his knee also. At the time and in my panic, I thought the white material was a bone. I ran to the house, burst through the door and raced to the phone breathlessly exclaiming to Rocke that I thought Race had broken his leg.

My hands were shaking so badly I couldn't even open the phonebook. Rocke took over, trying to figure out which Veterinary clinic was on call that night. In Pocatello, we only had two clinics that treated horses. The clinics traded weekends being on call for equine emergencies. That way, each doctor didn't have to take emergency calls so often. As it turned out, the clinic that was across the street from my mom's house was on call that night. I'd started taking all my horses to the other clinic in town when Race was a baby. At that point, in the middle of a winter night, I didn't care who we went to, as long as they could take care of Race.

We hastily hooked up the horse trailer, loaded him in and took off to the equine hospital. Upon our arrival, we discovered the Vet on call was a young man that I'd never met. He walked with a severe limp. He told us that he was essentially only a small animal Vet because of his injury. He told us that he had been accidentally shot ten years earlier and although he could walk, he was still very crippled.

He examined Race's wound and washed it. He then started the long process of debridement. This is the removal of the damaged tissue to improve the healing potential of the remaining healthy tissue. He also informed me that the white material was not a bone sticking out but a torn tendon. I was feeling calmer now that we were at the clinic and in the hands of a doctor.

I was just about to ask him how he was going to reattach the tendon when he used his surgical scissors and snipped it off. In surprise, I squeaked "Why did you just do that?" He assured me it would be okay. There was no way to mend it. It looked like a stick of string cheese that was halfway stripped. "The tendon" he said, "would regenerate itself." As he worked, I asked him if

Race would ever be sound again. He said he thought he had a good chance of it. And, as long as I didn't plan to barrel race him or anything else extreme like that, he would be healthy enough. *Somebody Scream!* Exasperated, I then informed him that was exactly what I'd intended to do with Race. He told me, in that case, we would just have to wait and see. With good luck and determined and dedicated rehabilitation efforts, he might heal well enough to compete in the athletically intense equine sport of barrel racing.

By the time the young Veterinarian had finished, he had placed over sixty sutures in the interior tissues and exterior hide of the knee wound. Hour after hour, layer after layer, he labored over the tedious reconstruction.

I felt sympathy for the young doctor. Because of the old gunshot injury, squatting down for hours sewing up Race's knee was excruciating for him. He would stagger up every once in a while, stretch and groan and then go back to work. I could tell he was in immense pain, but he did his job and did it well.

When we finally got home from the horse hospital, it was just about dawn. We were beat. Rocke was still sick and went straight back to bed. I wandered around the barn and corrals and tried to figure out what Race had caught his leg on to cause such a severe injury. I couldn't find anything.

The next day, I was having my morning coffee, sitting on the hearth of our fireplace that looked out over the backyard and arena. The floor to ceiling windows in the living room ran along the entire length of the room. I noticed big blotches of mud on the windows. Where the heck did those splatters come from?

I continued my investigation. As I looked out the window into the backyard, I finally saw the culprit---our 'in-the-ground' trampoline!   Rocke had been an accomplished trampolinist in college.   He even taught classes in trampoline at the local university. Every house we moved to, had to have a trampoline *in* the yard. We would dig a hole about six feet deep and the diameter of the tramp and install it in the ground. That way it was ground level. Then, all that our children and their friends would have to do was just step on. No shinnying up the frame to jump.

Well, what I finally figured out was this.   The horses, Race and Baile, had gotten out of the pasture somehow, possibly a loosely or unlatched gate.   They were probably trotting across the yard, Baile in the lead. I imagine that she saw the trampoline in front of her at the last moment and stepped to the side. Race was most likely close on her heels and didn't have time to veer after she did.   It appeared that he'd gone across the trampoline.   Obviously, trampolines are not built to withstand the weight and hooves of an 1100-pound horse. The springs broke, the jumping mat ripped and he fell through to the dugout area beneath.   As he struggled to climb out, a spring snagged the hide at his knee joint. The more he struggled, the more the sharp end of the spring tore into his skin. Evidently, the clamoring noise we heard that awoke us was Race breaking through and then struggling to get free of the trampoline.

We found springs all over the back yard. Some showed up in nearby trees, others as far as 40 feet away from the trampoline. I'm sure it was quite a sight, with missile like springs flying through the air! When we first built that house, we contemplated fencing the yard to keep children and dogs in. We never thought that we would need that fence to keep the horses out!

Race was at the animal hospital for about a week. The actual equine Veterinarian had taken over his care and she was confident that he would make a full recovery.

I visited him daily, sometimes more than once, and he finally came home. I continued with his care, changing bandages and administering medication. After the wound had healed and the stitches were removed, I treated the scar with Vitamin E oil. Since it was right on the knee joint, it was imperative that it heal soft and remain pliable. If it didn't heal correctly, he could be stiff in that knee for the rest of his life.

Race's knee did heal very well. The only remnant of that terrifying night was a "U" shaped scar that enveloped his entire knee joint.

Chapter 35

I started Race on barrels the spring of his four-year-old year. He was a fast learner and I was excited about his potential as a really excellent barrel horse. Unfortunately, I just could never get him "finished." He was too smart. Once he knew the pattern, he figured he didn't need to wait for my cue to turn the first barrel.

I tried everything I could think of to get him to wait on my cues. I would look way beyond the barrel, not even thinking about turning it, so that I didn't inadvertently cue him to turn. One time, I was in my arena working on my focus. I had to be absolutely clear in my intention of getting by that first barrel. I had to push him far enough past so that he could bend around without tipping it, rather than turning too soon and knocking it down with his shoulder. I was riding with all of my weight in the outside stirrup, hoping that I could hold him out far enough to make that turn. Rocke was working out in the yard and looked up just as I hit the dirt. Because all my weight was to the outside, when Race turned sharply into the barrel I was already half off. As I sat there in the dust, I felt the familiar nuzzle of Race's nose on my neck. It was as if he was saying "Why'd you get off?" Didn't Casey ask me that same question a few years ago? Rocke asked if I was alright. I was, but my ego was wounded again. I hadn't needed to ask for training help with any of my horses since I'd been ten years old! Why couldn't I finish Race into a barrel horse?

I tried putting race blinkers on him. I borrowed them from Chad. The blinkers consisted of a hood that fit over the horse's ears and had plastic cups on the outside of the openings for the horse's eyes. Because of these cups, the horse could only see straight ahead. Racehorses are often put in blinkers or blinders, so that the commotion of race day, big, noisy crowds and other horses, didn't distract them from the job at hand-- running a race. The first time I showed up at a jackpot with blinders on my barrel horse, I believe I was laughed at. I deserved to be. It was a ridiculous idea and it didn't work.

As I continued to struggle I took Race to a Barrel Racing Clinic being put on by a young successful barrel racer. Everyone "Oohed" and "Ahhed" over Race. He was so gorgeous and well put together. Again, the question of "Do you know what you have?" was asked. I said "Yes, I know I have a horse with all the potential in the world, but if I can't get him around the first barrel, I have nothing!" The clinic went well and Race did everything I asked of him. It seemed like we were making good headway; he was listening more to my leg cues and was allowing me to move him off the barrel before we turned. At the end of the day, a competition was held among the clinic participants. It was a chance to show off the new skills we'd developed and maybe win a little prize. We ran in to the arena and, as I cued him to widen his pocket at the first barrel he just blew by it and was out of control. I was so frustrated and embarrassed. The announcer made a point to tell me what a good job I was doing with a really tough horse. It was nice to hear, but didn't change the fact that I still couldn't finish a set of barrels.

I made arrangements to take him to the young woman that held the clinic for a month of barrel training. Maybe it was just me. Maybe he was so powerful and fast, that I was tensing up, or in some other way causing the problems. I hauled him the 150 miles to where the trainer lived. I put him in a paddock and told him I would be back in a few days to visit. I hated leaving him, but I figured I should give him one more chance to say yes to barrel racing. I visited three or four times during the month. Each visit, I saw a more beautiful and fit horse than the time before. One thing was for sure, he was being worked every day. When the thirty days were up, I drove over to bring him home. The trainer rode another horse and had me ride Race to see what I thought. I had always been able to get him to run a perfect set of barrels at three-quarter speed. It was when I kicked in the turbo boosters that it all fell apart. She had me slowly canter around the barrel pattern one time and then again a little faster. He ran them like he always did with me at less than top speed, perfect. When I asked her if he could do that at competition speed, she said "Well, I haven't really been able to get him there yet." Awesome! I just spent $600 to get my horse in really good shape.

I am embarrassed to admit that in my quest for perfection, I also used bigger, harsher bit and tie-down combinations and insistent spurs. None of which did anything but make me an abuser.   It saddens me to remember all that I put Race through. But, he still loved me; it is amazing what animals will let us do to them. I no longer wanted to do anything "to" him. I only wanted to do things "with" him.

It took me far too long to realize, that even though he had all of the physical attributes he needed to be a superstar athlete, barrel racing was not his destiny. I loved him much, much more than I loved running barrels, so I stopped trying to force him to be something he wasn't.   I just wish I would've grasped that understanding sooner.

By taking away the pressure and frustration that obtaining *my* goal was causing, and just taking a step back, I recognized what a true blessing just having him in my life was. We started just hanging out again, like we had when he was a baby. We began to rebuild that close connection that I'd almost sacrificed with my selfish ambition.

Chapter 36

I went to a couple of Natural Horsemanship clinics. The premise of Natural Horsemanship is to think, play and act like a horse. I liked the results I was getting by using some of the methods that were being taught. I'm not a groupie of one particular clinician, but I like to take bits and pieces from all of them and blend their techniques into a method that works for me and that my horses appreciate.

Within a few weeks of my newly re-found attitude, Race and I were on a magical path, one that we would travel together with lightness and grace. I threw out all of the old bits, tie-downs and other training gimmicks that I had in my tack room. I couldn't even sell them because I didn't want to be, however indirectly, the cause of another horse's pain and frustration. All I used now was a simple rope halter. That was all I needed on his head; Race was so light when not being forced into a high gear.

I took him to 4-H practice with Zack and Baile. He would stand around all night, allowing me to visit with other parents. Sometimes we would join the kids in the arena and I would coach them from horseback. Race was good with other horses and never caused any problems. He didn't bite or kick or ever pin an ear. He approached every horse and every kid as his friend, even Buddy the donkey (after the proper introduction had been made.)

I could ride him double with no problem. Baile on the other hand, hated having a second person sitting on her kidneys.   She would abide it, but only very begrudgingly and after a weak little tantrum buck-up.

Race was good in the arena, even if he thought we were going to run barrels again, he would just walk calmly into the arena. I still let him do the barrels at his speed; he and I both enjoyed that. He would walk along our road across from the elementary school, calm and cool, just enjoying being out and about the rural neighborhood. At the end of our road there were hay fields next to a dirt road with two tire tracks. I would practice his lateral movement on those tracks, and sometimes side-pass over the grassy median. The road was even enough that we could safely run with abandon, and that was always exhilarating for both of us.

Chapter 37

Life is good. I love those T-shirts, especially the one with the cool horse wearing sunglasses. Rocke and I were living the dream. It was 2004, and we'd just moved from Pocatello and our much-loved home, to Flower Mound, Texas near Dallas. Rocke had been given a job offer he just couldn't refuse and we were at a time in our lives, when a change was possible.

We hadn't even been looking for a change, so when the opportunity arose, we had to really do some soul searching to decide if we wanted to take advantage of the offer. I was teaching at the College of Technology at Idaho State University, in the same drafting program that I had graduated from in 1980, and Rocke had been with AMI, a semiconductor company, for over 20 years. Our jobs were secure and fulfilling, so why upset the apple cart so to speak?

The kids were grown. Our daughter, Jennifer was studying to be an equine Veterinarian, attending Vet school at Oregon State University. Our oldest son, TJ was attending Boise State University on a full ride scholarship for football, majoring in Business and Marketing (just like his dad) and our youngest, Zack, was just finishing up his senior year in high school. My mom had remarried after losing my dad to cancer nine years earlier.

There really was nothing holding us in Pocatello now, except habit. So, we took the leap. We broke the news to family and friends that we were flying the coop and starting a new chapter in our lives. We were moving to Texas! This news caused many a tear to be shed from our mothers, brothers and close friends. I told my good friend, Char over the phone while she was at work. She told me later that after that call, she calmly walked out of the office to the parking lot and climbed into her car. Then she just sat there and sobbed.

TJ and Jennifer seemed excited for us. Zack was going to move with us, so we wouldn't be totally lonely or completely empty nested.

Rocke moved in February to start his new job, while Zack finished his last semester of high school and I finished my contract year at the university.

Both Jennifer and TJ were getting married in mid-June. We planned our move around their weddings and Zack's high school graduation. To say June of 2004, was hectic and tremendously busy, would be an epic understatement.

The movers came and packed us up a few days before the week of the weddings. After the bright orange, 53 foot moving truck headed to Texas, Zack and I drove over to Boise to begin the wedding festivities. The truck arrived in Texas a couple of days later. Rocke and the movers hurriedly threw everything into the new house and garage. Rocke then caught a flight back to Idaho to join TJ for his bachelor party, whew!

The weddings were both lovely and memorable. TJ's was first and he was such a handsome groom. Jennifer's was the following weekend and she was an absolutely beautiful bride. We were all probably a little overly emotional because everyone knew this would be the last time we could just jump in the car and simply drive over to Boise for the weekend.

We said our goodbyes and gave a zillion hugs. Rocke flew back to Texas and Zack and I drove back to Pocatello to load up the horses, dogs and cat to start our cross country journey to our new home 1800 miles away. My friend Char was also going to make the drive with us. I think it was easier for both of us knowing we had an extra couple of weeks before our final goodbye.

It was important for me to have her see our new place in Texas, so when, in the future, we spoke on the phone, she could envision the places I'd be referring to in our conversations.

In addition to our horses, Race and Baile, the rest of our menagerie included Murphe and Cort, the dogs and Littlefoot, the cat. Cort was actually TJ's dog, but with his busy college life, he decided it was best that she live with us; she was a dachshund cross, black with little white tips on her toes. Murphe was our sweet German Shorthaired Pointer and Littlefoot was our tortoise colored cat. When the kids were young, we had a cat named Bigfoot, so when we adopted this kitten, Littlefoot seemed like a logical name.

Our plan was for our expedition to take four days and three nights. Jennifer had told me about HorseMotel.com and I'd made reservations with horse ranches along the way. Our journey was fairly uneventful, but we did have a few tense moments. About 150 miles into the trip we had our first blowout on a trailer tire. Fortunately, the horses were good and stood quietly, so that we didn't have to unload them on the freeway. Zack was able to get the blown tire changed and then we stopped in the next town, Brigham City, Utah and bought a replacement for the spare. We were back on the road in good time and made it to our first stop by early evening.

That first night, we stopped in Salina, Utah. The ranch was nice with a charming barn that had luxurious living quarters above. The owners were very friendly and accommodating. We joked that if their children were ever asked if they were raised in a barn they could reply "Why yes, yes we were!" Char and I took Race and Baile for a quick bareback ride around the grounds before we tucked them in to their stalls and left for our hotel. We figured they needed to stretch their legs after a long day in the trailer.

The moving truck driver was from Colorado and had advised us on the best route to take to Texas. He said "Whatever you do, don't go over Red Mountain Pass."

Char and I wanted to visit Pat Parelli's ranch in Pagosa Springs, Colorado on our way. I had an old map of my dad's, and I took the route that seemed the most direct to Durango and on to Pagosa. The route we took was the brightest line on that old, faded map, so I thought it was a main road. The problem with that road was it climbed right over an 11,000-foot mountain. You guessed it, Red Mountain Pass. I hadn't remembered the moving truck driver's advice about the daunting mountain when I decided which way we were going to go. I also didn't notice the light text showing the elevations on the map. As we started to crawl along the winding and very narrow road, Zack and I looked at each other, our eyes widening, as the realization hit us. We were on the very road we had been adamantly warned to avoid. At one particularly fear-provoking point, Char looked out the window and all she could see was thousands of feet down the side of the mountain. She just kept saying "Oh my god, oh my god." Zack finally offered to trade her places so she would be on the uphill side. They crawled over each other and switched seats. Just as Char got all settled and buckled in, the road followed a big switchback that caused her to be seated on the downhill side again. She buried her head in her hands and refused to look out for a few miles. The road was steep with many switchbacks all the way to the top and then all the way back down. It was a gorgeous drive, but extremely nerve racking. I was definitely a white knuckled driver!

On the bright side, since it was July, we were worried that the horses would be really hot in the trailer, but at 11,000 feet, the temperature was a mild 70 degrees. The cooler temps were good for us also. Our ten-year-old Chevy Suburban was working so hard to pull up the steep grade, we were afraid it might overheat, so, we didn't run the air conditioning. With the windows down, the cool, fragrant mountain air circulating through the truck was very refreshing.

I loved the smell of the mountains. It helped keep me calm and relaxed on that intense drive. Although Char and Zack both offered to take turns driving, I knew I'd be less stressed if I was in control of the fate of the horses. Whenever I ride with someone else pulling horses, I always feel that they're going too fast, taking turns too sharp and braking too hard.

We finally made it to Pagosa Springs, but too late. We stopped in at the Parelli Ranch only to find the gates closed. We were only able to drive in a little ways and see part of it. We had a reservation with a neighboring ranch for the horses; so we got them settled, then found a motel in town for us and the rest of the critters.

Pagosa Springs and Durango were both charming mountain towns. I wish we could've spent more time exploring that part of Colorado. But, we were on a schedule and Rocke was anxiously awaiting our arrival, so we got an early start the next morning and drove on.

On the third day of our journey, we had another blowout on the trailer, this time near Santa Rosa, New Mexico. Boy, were we happy it didn't happen the day before on that narrow, harrowing mountain road. We were able to find a small, decrepit old tire store that, incredibly, had the right sized trailer tire to again replace the spare.

One thing we discovered on that trip was that Cort, our little black dog, was camera shy. While we were driving, some of the views were so magnificent, we had to take pictures. On one of those occasions, Cort was sitting on Zack's lap in the front seat. Char handed him her camera so he could get a good shot of the breathtaking mountains. As Zack took the camera from Char, Cort scrambled to the back of the Suburban and dove under a blanket. What the heck? It was like she was shot out of gun. Zack took the picture and Char tried to coax Cort back to her. Cort was shaking like a leaf. We decided she must be in the witness protection program. From that moment on, whenever we pointed a camera at Cort, she scurried under the closest bed. It may have been the flash that originally freaked her out about having her picture taken. She hated flashlights and laser beams also. She certainly was a very special, one-of-kind little dog.

The last night of our journey, we stayed at a friend's place in Amarillo, Texas. As we drove into Amarillo, Zack noticed that many of the cars and trucks on the sales lots looked like someone had taken a baseball bat to their windshields. He questioned why anybody would do such a destructive thing. We mentioned it to our friends when we reached their home and they told us they'd just had a tornado a few days earlier. The tornado was accompanied by golf ball sized hail. The hail had done all of the damage to the windshields. Wow, that was just astounding and amazing. Welcome to Texas!

We were finally in Texas, so it seemed like we were getting close, but man, Texas is a big, big state. We got an early start and pulled into our new town by late afternoon on the fourth day of our trip.   We were exhausted and the animals were so ready to get out of the truck and trailer. We were home.

Chapter 38

Remember when I said Race needed a padded room? Well, his accident-proneness followed us to Texas. I had a steel harrow that I used to work up my arena in Idaho. I was using it to spread manure and stimulate the ground in the new pastures. I'd leaned it up against the fence and secured it inside the pasture. It was out of the way and I didn't believe it posed any danger. One of the few things we absolutely hated about Texas was the fire ants. Those little bastards were everywhere. Shortly before we had any intention of moving, I'd read an article about fire ants and what a nuisance they were in the south. I chuckled to myself and thought "I'm sure glad we don't have fire ants to contend with in Idaho." The joke was on me.

Back to Race; He was standing with his back to the fence, resting in the shade of the barn. Evidently, he was stomping his feet, trying to get the pesky fire ants off his legs, when he struck an edge of the harrow. My home office was just outside his pasture. As I worked at my computer, I saw him standing by the fence with one back leg cocked. It looked like he was napping. A girl who had been walking her dog on the road noticed him. She came to my door and asked if I knew my horse was bleeding. What? No! I hurried out to take a look. Bleeding was an understatement; he was standing in a puddle of blood. I thanked her profusely for taking the time to stop and tell me. Thank goodness for the kindness of strangers!

First, I ran to the house and got an oversized bath towel and an ace bandage to wrap around his leg. Then, as I was frantically hooking up the horse trailer, I called the Vet to make sure there was a doctor at the clinic. By the time I'd gotten the trailer hooked up and had run back to the barn to get Race, blood had soaked clear through the bath towel. Rather than take the time to wrap it again, I just loaded him quickly, (Yea! for his good loading manners), and drove to the clinic. The Veterinary Technician immediately started running very cold water over the wound to try to reduce the bleeding. Once the gushing had been slowed, the Vet started the, all too familiar task of stitching Race up. Oh, how that boy could find the one thing on the whole place that could hurt him! I was seriously considering building him that padded stall!

*****

In 1999, Chad asked me if I would be willing to sell Chachi to Chuck (the youngest Price boy) for his oldest daughter to compete on in high school rodeo. Chuck's wife was a barrel racer and had several nice, young, high powered horses coming along, but they wanted a seasoned veteran to carry their daughter safely around the barrel course and still be competitive enough to have success. Chachi was a perfect choice.

I hadn't planned to sell him, ever. But since I was spending so much time with Race, he wasn't being used to his potential. He had lost a step with age and wasn't able to post the times necessary to keep winning at the professional level. I reluctantly and hesitantly agreed to sell him to Chuck's family. As I stood in the barn brushing him before Chad came to pick us up to haul him down to Elko, Nevada to his new home, tears were streaming down my face. Zack came out, put his arm around me and said "Mom, you don't have to sell him, why don't you just say no?" I told him that it would probably be better for Chachi to be used more and continue to do what he loved. We should at least let them give him a try.

When we delivered him to Chuck, I wouldn't even let them pay me for him yet. I was quietly hoping they would decide he wouldn't work out for what they needed and send him back home.

Of course they loved him and sent me the check. Over the next ten years, in addition to his oldest daughter, Chuck's son and young twin daughters used Chachi for Junior Rodeo and jackpots. I believe they won quite a bit of money, many year-end awards and even a saddle or two. I'd asked Chad to tell them that whenever they were ready to retire Chachi, he would always have a home with me. I really wanted to stop in Elko on our way to Texas and pick him up.

Chad called and told me "Chuck said you can have that horse back." Unfortunately, that call didn't come from Chad until after we'd been in Texas for a while. By that time, I had realized how astronomically expensive it was to keep horses in Texas. It also didn't seem prudent to drive 1300 miles, each way, to go get him.

I've always regretted not bringing Chachi home to live out the rest of his days with me. I wanted him to know that he was loved and appreciated for all of the wonderful times he had given to so many.

I *hate* regrets.

******

Chapter 39

We were enjoying our new life and each other. When you move away from everyone and everything familiar, you realize you must depend on each other more than ever. Rocke and I treasured this new phase of our lives. We lived on Pepperport Lane in Flower Mound, Texas, I loved the sound of our colorful new address, Oh, and our zip code was 75022. There was that number again!

One day, I was out riding Race around the pasture. Other than going down our dead-end road, I really hadn't discovered any other places to ride yet. A woman on a cute little dun mare was riding down the road. I galloped over to the fence and said "Hi, my name is Susan. We just moved here from Idaho and I need someone to ride with! Will you be my friend?" That silly little conversation was the beginning of a wonderful friendship, Kim and I became instant friends. I introduced her to Natural Horsemanship and helped her with a few issues she was having with her other horse, a gelding she called Blazer. She showed me some great equestrian trails around the many lakes in the Dallas area. We went to numerous horse shows and events held at the Will Rogers Coliseum in Fort Worth. That was one of the best things about Texas; there was never a shortage of horse activities to watch or in which to participate.

At first everything seemed to be going well in our new home. We had a very nice four-stall barn and three acres of pasture, which in Idaho would have been plenty of pasture for two horses...but not in Texas. After about a month, we realized the horses were losing weight at an astonishing rate. I didn't understand; there were lots of fat healthy horses in Texas. After endless research, I realized the Texas pasture grass just didn't have the nutrients that were found in the lush, irrigated pasture grass in Idaho. Nutrients, that my horses were used to and obviously needed. So, I started on the long, and very expensive, road to put the weight back on them. Jennifer, my daughter who was now an equine Veterinarian in Oregon, told me to feed Race and Baile a Senior Horse Feed as it could be used as a total feed or as a supplement. Even though my horses weren't considered senior horses yet, they were only 11 and 12 years old respectively, she thought it would do them good.

It seemed as though I was feeding the horses an immense amount of extra feed. They were still not doing well on the coastal hay and supplemental feed mix. When we first got to Texas and I started inquiring about hay, I was told that I shouldn't feed alfalfa that had been grown in the South, to my horses. There was an insect called a Blister Beetle that nested in alfalfa fields. These beetles don't affect cattle, but they are fatal to horses if ingested. The horse's mouth, lips and throat swell so quickly and severely that the horse suffocates within hours. Thinking there was no way to get good alfalfa from up north, say from Idaho, I just kept feeding them the coastal nutrient-free hay and dollar bills. Well, not really, but the amount I was spending on supplemental feed was astronomical and it made it seem like that's what I was doing!

After listening to my ongoing rants about the horrible grass and hay in Texas, Jennifer finally said, "Can't you get them alfalfa?" That was what they were used to and evidently that's what they still needed. She said "Feed them steak, (alfalfa)...a diet of all coastal hay was like a diet of straight mashed potatoes." So, with some very determined perseverance, I found a source of alfalfa hay that had been shipped in from Wyoming. After two years of frustration, it seemed my special, but skinny horses were finally going to be on the road to recovery.

They were so happy, their eyes and noses knew exactly what we were stacking in the barn. The return to health was happening. They were both gaining weight and their coats were finally returning to the silken, lustrous sheen they'd always had in Idaho.

Chapter 40

On a beautiful autumn day, I had been riding Race and practicing every other step flying lead changes down in my neighbor's arena (Texans really are exceptionally nice and generous people). I had Race doing these lead changes the entire length of the arena. We had been playing at bridle-less riding also and everything was grand. It was such a bright, beautiful day, unseasonably warm, but not too hot. He was doing so well that I did one more round of lead changes and headed home.

After giving Race a much deserved bath, I just hung out with him around the house loving on him. This had become our usual ritual every evening, just spending nice relaxing time together. After giving up barrel racing, I realized how really burned out I was with the highly competitive sport. I was so enjoying the stress-free life of not competing and the sheer joy of just having a horse in my life, with no expectations other than companionship and happiness.

The next morning, October 1, 2006, (I will never forget that date) I went out to feed Baile and Race. Baile immediately came in from the pasture to her stall for breakfast, but not Race. I asked Baile "Where's your partner?" I found him standing behind the barn, very lethargic and low headed. I led him into his stall and offered him some pellets. He wasn't interested. I called my Vet, who was also my next door neighbor, but he was out of state at an annual Equine Veterinary Conference. He gave me the Lone Star Park Emergency Clinic's phone number. I called and relayed Race's symptoms and told them we were on our way.

It was an hour and a half drive and by the time we got there, Race seemed a little better. The Vet on call was a young Scotsman and was fresh out of school, but seemed competent. He couldn't find any obstruction, but said Race was severely dehydrated so they would keep him over night on IV fluids and he would probably be fine by morning and we could come back and get him then. He gave me his cell number and said he would answer right away if I wanted to call back later and check on Race. I patted Race on the neck and told him I would see him tomorrow...

I called about 6:00 that evening but he didn't answer, so I just left a message and suggested that if Race was doing well enough, maybe I could come back and pick him up that evening. I hated not having Race home even for one day. The young Vet called me back at about 8:45 and apologized for not answering. He said they had another horse come in with severe colic and that horse was not doing well at all. He said, with a very strong Scottish accent "Your big guy is doin' great, he's just resting in his stall...If ya' still want to come an' get him, ya' can." Since it was more than an hour drive and close to 9 pm, I said that we would just come back, as planned, in the morning.

I was so relieved and my spirits were high. I thought everything was well and looked forward to seeing Race in the morning and bringing him home.

My phone rang at 10:30pm and I knew immediately I didn't want to answer. My stomach sunk, my hands were shaking, I knew something had happened. When I warily answered the phone, the Vet said "Susan, I am so sorry, Race just died..."

As I am recounting that horrible night, the tears are streaming down my face and I feel sick all over again. The rest of that night is a blur...my husband and son trying to console me. Me, trying to make sense out of it.

The next morning, Rocke went back to the clinic to pick up the trailer and make the arrangements for Race's burial. I said I should go with him, but he said "There is absolutely no reason to put yourself through that, I'll take care of it." My wonderful, thoughtful husband.

The reason for Race's death was never determined. When they performed the necropsy they found a laceration in his stomach, but had no explanation of what caused it. I thought about back when Race was a yearling and his sire suddenly died, could there have been something genetically wrong? We will never know. Still, to this day, I wonder if I did something to cause his death, that one last round of lead changes, was it too hot? Did he need more water during our ride? Were there signs of distress after we got home that I should have noticed?

I felt my world had just crumbled around me. I walked around in a daze for the first few days after Race died. I took Cort and our new German Shorthaired Pointer puppy, Annie, for walks down the road. If my neighbors saw me, they would come out and hug me and try to comfort me. The problem was I was inconsolable.

When my neighbor, Bob, who was my regular Veterinarian got home, he called and said "Susan, I only see one horse in your pasture." I sobbed into the phone "Race died!" I then had to throw the phone to Rocke. I could get no more words out. Rocke told him the entire unbelievable story. Bob was so upset he immediately called the emergency clinic to find out what had happened with Race. I don't think he was given much more information than we were. He also made a generous donation in Race's name to the Texas A&M School of Veterinary Medicine. It was a very thoughtful thing to do. I don't know if anything would have been different if he'd been home that Saturday. I think he wondered, too, if he could have done something more that would have saved Race.

All of my family, friends and neighbors were so kind and supportive, but I just could not get over Race's death. After a while people started saying "You have to move on, he was just a horse." It had been six months and that was just it, he was not "just a horse." He was *my* horse...my special, wonderful love of a horse...*my beautiful boy.*

My family was happy and healthy, the rest of my pets were happy and healthy. Life is good, right? The shirt says so. So, why was I still so sad and depressed?

What kind of therapy did I need to help me move on? How could I dig out of this sadness and despair?

Friends suggested I should get another horse. I didn't want another horse, I wanted Race. Every time I looked out in the field, there was Baile, despondent and miserable with her head held low. She was just as sad and brokenhearted as I. Baile was a yearling when I got Race. She and Race had been together for 13 years and now she was alone for the first time in her life.

As I struggled to recover, I kept thinking of Race and all of the other horses I'd loved in my life. The more I thought of them, the more it seemed that I had some kind of responsibility to tell their stories. So, I started writing.

It seemed to be the therapy I needed. As I wrote, I cried. I called old friends to clarify memories and that helped too. Finally, I could see the light. I felt myself starting to heal and return to my old self.

But, Baile wasn't healing; she was still sad and alone in the pasture

EPILOGUE

So, to make a long story a little longer, I decided to get Baile and myself a new horse. I drove over 3000 miles looking at horses from Oklahoma City to Austin, Texas and everywhere in between.

I tried finding a horse from the Dash For Cash line, but realized none of them would be good enough. None of them would be Race.

I saw an ad for a nice looking yearling colt, and made plans to go take a look at him in late December, but the day before, Annie, my pup, had caught her skin on a wire at the neighbor's arena while I was riding Baile and ripped her side open. As it so happens, that neighbor, Tim, was our dog and cat Vet. His wife drove me with Annie, bleeding on my lap, to his clinic. I just left Baile loose in their arena. We left Annie at the clinic in the expert hands of the Vet and returned to the arena to get Baile and go home. Tim brought Annie home with him that evening and dropped her off to me. He had placed two layers of sutures in her side. She would be fine, but since I needed to stay home and take care of her, I delayed going to look at the yearling.

I was finally able to arrange to go see the yearling in early spring. Now, he was a two-year-old. I really liked the looks of him and said I was definitely interested and I would keep him in mind. I had driven about four hours south to look at the colt. I was so close to Austin, I decided to stop at a race horse rescue farm that I'd read about. I thought I might as well see if they had any horses that might appeal to me.

I looked at some of the retired Thoroughbred racehorses that had been surrendered to them, but none of them seemed to be what I wanted. After relaying what type of horse I was looking for, the owner of the farm told me she was expecting to get a Quarter Horse gelding in soon. She would call me when he arrived.

A couple of weeks later, she called and I drove back down to look at him. I really liked him, but was worried about his soundness. He hadn't been Vet checked yet, but she said their Vet would be out soon.

On my way back home, I decided to stop back in and take one more look at the two-year-old colt I liked. He was just back from being gelded and after seeing him again, I realized just how much I liked him, so I told the seller I wanted the colt and I would talk to my husband and we would come back on the weekend to pick him up. I emailed him and asked numerous questions as to what kind of hay and feed he was used to, whether he was up-to-date on vaccinations and de-worming and expressed my excitement about buying him. I didn't hear from him all week and sent him another couple of emails trying to arrange the details of the purchase. I was starting to get a little irritated. When I finally received a response to my emails, it simply stated, "I'm sorry, that colt has been sold." Seriously? Evidently, I should have paid for him right then. I think he must've used my offer to drive up the price to another prospective buyer. I was pretty disappointed, I had looked at a lot of horses and he was the only one that felt right.

I did really like the Quarter Horse at the rescue facility in Austin. I told myself and Rocke, "It must be fate, maybe I was supposed to get this one all along." I decided to take a chance on him, even though his feet seemed quite sore. The rescue operator assured me it was a shoeing issue and she'd had him checked over by their Vet. So, I paid the $900 adoption fee and made plans to come back the following weekend to pick him up. Rocke drove down to Austin with me. He liked his looks and we both felt good about getting a rescue horse.

.

*** 2006 ***

When Rocke brought the horse trailer back from the Lone Star Clinic the day after Race died, Baile whinnied and whinnied. She just kept pacing, waiting for us to unload Race and put him back in the field with her, it was heartbreaking to watch.

As time went on, she would still always look up when a white horse trailer would drive by, but, I think she knew, Race wasn't coming home.

******

This time, the white horse trailer did pull in to our place. *This time*, Baile ran to the fence and whinnied with bright eyes and pricked up ears, just like she had that sad, sad day last October. *This time*, we unloaded a handsome bay horse. She was thrilled. We put the gelding in the corral and let them get acquainted over the fence. After the initial, "I'm the boss of you!" mare squeal from Baile, they acted like long lost friends. She was so happy to have a pasture mate again.

I decided to call him Handsome Rob, after the charming character from the movie *The Italian Job*. Another, more personal reason for the name was Race's initials were ROB. Remember, his registered name was Racing On By.

A couple of days after we got him home, I asked my Vet/next door neighbor Bob, if he would take a look at him, just to make sure there wasn't something wrong with him beyond his sore feet. I had already started to become seriously attached and so had Baile. But, as I tried to work with him, he just didn't seem right.

I slowly walked him next door, and Bob watched as Handsome Rob haltingly made his way through the pasture. I could tell by the look on Bob's face, that he was immediately concerned. He poked and prodded, stretched his legs and neck. Then, he pushed on the side of his neck and the gelding nearly fell down. He did it from the other side, with the same results. He said "I hate to do this to you, Susan, but I think you better take him back. He has something seriously wrong, neurologically." He told me I could never ride him safely because he could fall at any time. He thought the horse must have had a severe injury to his neck or back sometime in his life.

My spirit was crushed again...I couldn't bear the thought of taking him away from Baile. She was just starting to be her old self again. But, I also couldn't afford to just keep him as a pet. Though it was overwhelmingly hard, I called the rescue operator, and gave her the news that I would be returning this sweet, sweet gelding. She wasn't very cooperative, which made it even harder. Zack went with me to return him to Austin. I didn't think I could take much more. Even though I'd only had him for a week or so, I felt a tremendous loss.

I thought "It shouldn't be this hard to find the right horse." What should have been an exciting time was causing me more anxiety than I could handle. Maybe I was not yet ready to get another horse after all.

I was on the verge of putting my horse search on hold for a while when I came across a picture on the internet of a breathtaking Thoroughbred. The photo was fuzzy and dark, but I could see enough. I remember calling Zack in to the room to look at the picture. I said "Zack, I think I've found him."

So, I drove up to Oklahoma City one more time and shook up my horse ideals by purchasing an off-the-track Thoroughbred (OTTB).

White's Bonus Time is the great, great, grandson of Secretariat. He raced for three years and had one "Win" photo. I guess that's why he was "off the track!"

I bought Bonus when he was five years old. He may not be Race...no horse ever will be. But he is a beautiful, charming and extraordinary horse. And through his challenges, love and endless play, Baile and I have returned.

I feel that the universe had something to do with me finding Bonus. I believe his name is providence. He is my bonus horse.

I built two headstones for Race. One for his grave site and one to keep with me. Mine is in a special place in our yard under a grand old pine tree. As I pass by that simple monument on my way to the barn, I say "Hi Racy Roo" and fondly think of Race. Then, I see the ever charismatic Bonus, watching for me with his bright, beautiful, brown eyes, and I think, "Oh no, I've done it again. I've fallen in love with another magnificent horse."

But that's another story.

Race's Gravestone-Pine Hill Cemetery in Bowie, Texas

RACING ON BY
April 16, 1993-October 1, 2006
My Big, Beautiful Boy

RACE,
Thank You for Your Gentle Heart,
Your Endless Try and
Your Kind and Loyal Spirit
You Will Be With Me Always...
I'll Hear Your Nicker in the Wind and
Feel Your Strength Within Me

ABOUT THE AUTHOR

Susan Acree and
White's Bonus Time

Susan's memoir of loss and love comes from her life-long journey with horses. Her trials and adventures will touch the heart of anyone who has experienced an extraordinary relationship with a special horse.

She has been blessed throughout her life with many wonderful horses, and though she lost her deeply loved Race, her journey continues. She and her husband live in Idaho.

In addition to *The Horses I've Loved, A Memoir,* Susan is the author of *Our Bonus Horse, The True Story of a Charming, yet Challenging Off Track Thoroughbred Who Healed Two Hearts.* She is also the creator of the Bonus and Baile Cartoon Series and Buck and Gil's Travelling Blog.

Find them all at www.thethirstyzebra.com

Acknowledgements

Thank you to my friends and family members that allowed me to impose on them for editing and opinions during the writing of this book.

Thanks too, to my husband, my children and my mother for a lifetime of unconditional love and support.

I would also like to thank Pam Mosbrucker for her invaluable instruction, advice and motivation.

Thirsty Zebra
Publishing

Made in the USA
Coppell, TX
19 February 2020

16003342R00138